Confidence & Assertiveness for Women

The Female Guide to Gaining Confidence, Self-Esteem and Assertiveness

Kate Garner

Table of Contents

Introduction

I am a woman and my daily experiences require me to be bold. From the moment I open my eyes in the morning, I am expected to fearlessly concern myself with the needs of my family. During the day when I have free-time for myself, I am bombarded with negative self-talk in my mind, telling me to make greater leaps in my professional life. In the evenings when my family has been fed, the home swept clean, and everyone is winding down, I sit alone in a bathtub of bubbles wondering whether I had accomplished all that I could on that particular day. As a woman, I feel the persistent pressure to have control over my life and in some miraculous way, align my personal life with my professional life. Indeed, like many women in the world, I am seeking to achieve the abstract goal of balance whereby I feel complete with all parts within and around me.

The goal of achieving balance is not desirable on its own. Along with balance, I find that women desire peace at home and at work. The longing for peace has been at the forefront of women's movements throughout time. Historically and politically, women have always been the subsidiaries in our global society. We have been the objects of control in our households and our public lives. Most of the grievances that women are burdened with are based on the notable inequality between men and women. This inequality between the genders inevitably causes much suffering for women. One of the greatest manifestations of gender inequality has been the imbalance of power and resources.

Disempowered women are oppressed women, regardless of their social class. This is because with power comes privilege, and therefore the lack of power that women are given creates marginalization or the assumption of a secondary position in society. Without power, women find it challenging to be bold even when their daily experiences require it of them. The first attack that women face is the socio-economic one, which is experienced through institutional and social barriers that have barred women from accessing positions of influence and power. This has caused suffering because it has negatively impacted on the work prospects of women, causing them to aim for lower paying jobs or accept a fraction of the pay that men are given at work.

Secondly, women are attacked psychologically. This kind of attack is experienced internally and it is a product of a woman's external reality. For instance, when we are marginalized in our communities and workplaces, we are forced to accept the role of the lesser and consent to living a life in the shadows of those who have more power than us. When we are stripped of our power as women, our voice or freedom of expression is taken away from us too. Yes, even though technically we are allowed to voice our beliefs, opinions, and fears, we come to accept that our voice has been muted by those at the forefront of decision-making; those who are always men more powerful than us. The consequence of feeling powerless and not being able to voice our suffering has caused psychological pain.

The most potent emotion which comes to mind when I think about the psychological impact of being disempowered is fear. Women have felt and lived through fear for many generations. I always think of fear as being a double portion of grief; not only are we terrified by the imaginary hand of punishment in our environments that could potentially cause us to stumble, we are also terrified by our own ambitions, dreams, and calls to be bold, which would cause us to be seen and therefore become a target for this punishment. In other words, we fear the oppressive nature of society toward women, which creates barriers to our success and furthermore, we fear our own call to action which is the voice inside our head that tells us to go out into the world and be extraordinary.

I wrote this book for women like me who have experienced hardships, not only in progressing in their professional careers, but also in owning their power at home and within intimate relationships. This book is an offering to begin the process of healing in your life by investigating the many fears that have stopped you from claiming the power that is within your control. Indeed, as women, we have been dealt with unfavorable cards, however, I am determined to show you that even with your unfavorable cards you can continue to progress in your life. One of the significant themes that I would like to present to you in this book are the themes of inner confidence and assertiveness.

Inner confidence is the ability to believe that you have the best intentions for your life and that you are able to choose the best course of action in your life. Inner confidence is a necessary quality for all women because it is what allows us to dare to be great. In a world where women are not seen, your confidence will give you the ability to trust in your plan and rely on the talents and skills which you have honed over the years to assist you in reaching the milestones that you have set.

A lack of confidence has adverse effects. When you lack inner confidence, there is a noticeable stagnation that you experience in your life. This stagnation is not necessarily caused by a lack of initiative or clear goals to achieve the success you desire. Instead, this stagnation is a result of the lack of assurance that you have in your own ability to start something and complete it effectively. One again, it is the psychological attack of fear which causes you to see yourself as being small and unable to challenge societal systems that seem more powerful than you are.

The second theme which I will present to you in this book is the theme of assertiveness. An assertive woman is an empowered woman. I would describe assertiveness as the act of standing up for your values, beliefs, and desires in a way that inspires confidence. Contrary to what most people believe, assertiveness is not synonymous with aggression. In other words, an assertive woman does not need to be an angry woman. Rather, she is able to stand up for justice, truth, and fairness with strength that does not seek to attack. Furthermore, an assertive woman is one who seeks to find her voice again and express it with boldness. Many of us have choked when we had to speak up for ourselves and set boundaries with others. Perhaps it was our own feelings of being rejected or misunderstood that stood in our way.

Nonetheless, learning how to be assertive will teach you that it is okay to express what you are experiencing, both inwardly and outwardly. In fact, by sharing your lived reality with others in a non-threatening way, you would be giving others insight into how you are experiencing the world and how the actions of others are affecting you. Speaking up should not be a fearful exercise that you dread; it should instead become an opportunity for you to share your concerns, fears, and experienced difficulties with those in power or positions of influence. Without having the confidence to voice how you are feeling, you cannot influence the behaviors or actions of those who may be oppressing you. Your verbal and non-verbal communication will send a clear message to those who have the power to make changes.

To illustrate some of the points that I will make in this book, I will draw upon my own experiences of helplessness which ultimately led me to find my own strength. Although I would call myself a confident woman now, I was not always this fearless. It took me many years of people-pleasing and being afraid of stepping out in my own power to fully come to a place of self-acceptance. Even though I was undermined at work and undervalued at home, I could not lie to myself anymore and think that my suffering was a result of my environment alone. The truth is that I was also contributing to the suffering that I was experiencing in my life by silencing my own voice too. I had big dreams like becoming an author but I was afraid to entertain my dreams long enough to act on them. In essence, I was oppressing myself by placing limits on who I can be and what I can do in this short life that I have.

It was my decision to regain the lost power that had been taken from me and that which I willingly gave away, that led me to a place of healing and finding my confidence. In this book, I intend to lead you to the same realization that I had experienced in order for you to find your confidence and assertiveness too. No longer will you have to feel smaller or less intelligent than a man at work or at home, and no longer will you label yourself as an angry woman. My hope is to share my own truth and the knowledge which I have acquired through years of inquiry to direct you on your own path of truth too. In the end, you will have learned how to be a bold and fearless woman who views the world with a heart full of love and a mind ready to conquer every trial presented to you with grace.

Part One:

Getting Ready to Make a Change

Chapter One:

What is Female Confidence and

Assertiveness?

"Staying silent is like a slow growing cancer to the soul and a trait of a true coward. There is nothing intelligent about not standing up for yourself. You may not win every battle. However, everyone will at least know what you stood for—YOU."

– Shannon L. Alder

Even when the power that you have as a woman is denied, your indispensable presence is still felt. Over the years, I have seen many examples of powerful women both young and old who have committed themselves to work and made a resolution to not quit until their goals materialized. Our competence has been seen in the rising number of young female graduates who are taking up space in the corporate world and making their mark. For the first time in our collective history, women are filling the workforce and beginning to occupy positions of power in middle level management. Even more, company executives are starting to see the value of a workforce full of women in the increased performance and profitability of influential companies.

However, it is alarming to find that in these same companies, the efforts of women receive mere recognition but those of men are rewarded with promotions and raises. How can it be that in a society full of hardworking and talented women, it is still the performance of men that is recognized as being impressive and worthy of unquestionable salary increases? What is it that women are not doing or that executives are refusing to acknowledge? Unfortunately, as talented as women professionals are, there is still marginal representation of women executives in most corporate firms. Over half a century since women forced their way into the office, our capabilities are still under review.

Women are part of the invincible workforce whose contributions are looked down upon. It should not be surprising to you then that many women underplay or undervalue their own contributions at work. Think about the last time you received a promotion. When it came, did you feel as though it was well deserved? Or how did you celebrate this amazing milestone (if any celebration was had in the first place)? I have had many conversations with women from all levels of the organization hierarchy and none of the discussions left me as speechless as I was when I spoke to the women in senior levels of management. My expectation when I asked them to share their thoughts about being part of management was that they would be thrilled at finally being noticed for their brilliance. However, the responses that I received showed that the women executives doubted their own capabilities and fit for their position.

Even though they had admittedly gone to the best colleges and had an impressive track record of being high performers, I noticed a glimpse of a lack of confidence and this made me quite sad. All of this time, I imagined that the fight against gender inequality would be won when women assumed positions of leadership. However, from my discussions with influential women in powerful positions, I found that the fight against gender inequality was rooted deeper. The real war would be won when women began to see themselves and their contributions in the workplace and at home as being valuable and deserving of honor. The battle was on the level of self-perception and how we—as women—could pick up the shattered pieces of our self-esteem and maximize our potential to succeed among men in our various industries.

Confidence Gap Theory

There are many disparities between men and women at work. For instance, it is common to find disparities in salaries, executive appointments, or even roles of governance. Nonetheless, I find that there is no disparity more striking than the level of confidence between the two sexes. There have been many studies that have shown that women are less confident in their work capabilities than men are and as a result of this self-doubt, women were less likely to boldly request promotions at work or stand up for themselves when faced with extremely unfair practices. The lack of self-advocacy was seen to justify the fear of negative repercussions that would follow from standing up for themselves.

I am sure you can relate to this research to some degree. It is so common for women to choose to fade in the background because going unnoticed is perceived as being safe. This fear is not imagined or part of a workforce disillusionment. Rather, it is a manifestation of years of marginalization that women have experienced, being sidelined and inhibited from competing with men economically. Now that more women are allowed to compete, many of us still need to heal from a damaged psyche due to centuries of being told that we could not lead. The disparities in confidence between men and women in the workplace is what we know as the confidence gap theory, and if you ask me, I believe that the confidence gap has more devastating ramifications than the closing gender gap.

Nowadays, it is rare to see spaces where women are prohibited access due to the lack of skills or talents. I would go as far as saying that men and women are presented similar opportunities in terms of receiving a quality education. If there are no gaps in the access to educational opportunities, why then are we still seeing boards with no female representation at all? I believe that the confidence gap theory can give us a reasonable answer. When women feel as though they are less qualified to lead when pitted against a fellow male colleague of the same educational background, they will shrink or minimize their value when it comes to pitching for a promotion. You see, it becomes less about the access to power and more about the low self-perception that the woman carries which reinforces her powerlessness.

In other words, men may also carry doubts about career prospects, however, they are still willing and courageous enough to fight for apparent opportunities. Women on the other hand, are less likely to break through glass ceilings or take bold risks in their professional lives because of how low we perceive our own power to lead, make decisions, be the frontrunner in a team, or work together with senior authorities. The reality is that an under qualified male will lift his chest and walk into a meeting with his frontline manager to discuss possibilities of a salary increase, yet the overqualified and high performing woman will still worry about how the frontline manager will perceive her request and whether the demand for her overdue salary increase will sound too greedy or ungrateful.

The term that we use for women who feel as though they do not deserve their work position is imposter syndrome. You will know when you are suffering with the imposter syndrome because it usually carries with it a deep sense of doubt about your own contributions and accomplishments. You feel as though your success was a mistake or that it happened by chance. Those who suffer with imposter syndrome are fearful of being caught out for their perceived shortcomings. This psychological pattern will make you feel fraudulent for being promoted high above the rank that you would be comfortable working in. In your mind, you are still not ready for that promotion or to change career fields and pursue your dream job; in other words, those with imposter syndrome readily undermine their own efforts or ambitions.

What is Assertiveness for Women?

The refusal for women to be their own advocate in their private and public lives is to me, a form of self-sabotage. I call it self-sabotage because we protest for our freedom yet our minds remain chained to the memory of being disempowered. Hewlett-Packard conducted a fascinating research on the ways to get women positions into senior level management many years ago (Kay & Shipman, 2014). In their research, they found that women who worked at the company only applied for a promotion when they believed to have met 100% of the criteria and requirements of the job post. On the contrary, men who worked in the company were eager to apply for the post when they believed to have met only 60% of the criteria and requirements.

This research shows us a frightening reality of life in the corporate environment for an average woman. It shows us that women erect self-imposed barriers between where they are positioned in the company currently, and where they desire to be positioned in the future. The only time when an average woman working in the corporate environment would feel confident in their skills and abilities is when they have reached some level of perfection. Indeed, we set our performance bar so high that most of the time we feel like failures because we cannot reach it. At some point we need to come to the realization that when we underestimate our own abilities it is not a display of modesty, but rather a demonstration of a lack of assertiveness.

By definition, assertiveness refers to the ability to express your truth openly with others and to take bold action, knowing that you are confident in the outcomes. It describes living your life audaciously without any fear of being punished for being authentic to who you are. People pleasers have a difficult time being assertive because of the debilitating fear of being judged or alienated for expressing their opinions or thoughts. I understand this fear because for a long time I was a people pleaser too. I entered and left the corporate environment without ever expressing any grievance that I had with my coworkers to those in positions of power who could have helped me solve my disputes. I was terrified of being the office outcast from expressing my hurt to others. I perceived voicing my opinions as being confrontational and feared that it may lead to more trouble. My lack of assertiveness at work is perhaps one of the contributing factors to my dissatisfaction with my job and those I worked with.

My default of smiling and nodding did not pay off at the end—it left me unemployed and full of resentment. I was agreeable to a fault, and even though I had intelligent remarks to make, none of them ever left the safety of my mind. When I learned to become more assertive, I was already without a job, however, it changed how I perceive my power in any given moment. I began to learn how to speak with the same clarity of thoughts and ideas that I had. I began to imagine myself sounding more confident speaking my truth and genuinely believing that what I had to share with others was insightful and meaningful. Furthermore, I committed to quit undermining my own thought processes, assumptions, opinions or the way I interpreted things.

I started to see that assertiveness has no association with aggressiveness at all. It wasn't a free ticket to bully others or to arrogantly proclaim my thoughts and feelings. I learned that assertiveness was actually a way for me to respect and honor my own rights without finding a need to stifle those of others. Without the luxury of a corporate job to practice my new found assertiveness, I thought of all the other ways that I could be assertive in my personal life. I began to think of all the many goals I had planned to accomplish in the future and after much deliberation, I decided to be assertive about accomplishing one of them. I chose to focus on the goal of becoming an author and sharing my knowledge and truth through written words to an audience of readers across the world.

Becoming assertive about working toward this goal required a certain level of commitment that I needed to make with myself. Yes, I needed to make a commitment with myself that I would continue to strive to attain this goal until it would eventually happen. I could not later decide to quit or waste valuable time waffling or deliberating never-ending plans—this would be a way of undermining my own commitment and thus withdrawing to a place of fear. I was bold in my declaration that either I was going to be all in or not bother seeking to accomplish this goal at all.

After many years, my relentless and assertive attitude paid off. Not only was I an author, but I was also writing a book about the very wisdom that had helped me to experience life with a fresh mindset. What I have found throughout my journey of unlearning most of the self-deprecating and negative programming that we are taught as women, is that our confidence and assertiveness reveal opportunities within our midst that we were not aware of before we decided to let go of the mental strongholds that seek to pull us down.

Chapter Two:

Understanding Common Factors

that Hold Women Back

"Whether I am meant to or not, I challenge assumptions about women. I do make some people uncomfortable, which I'm well aware of, but that's just part of coming to grips with what I believe is still one of the most important pieces of unfinished business in human history— empowering women to be able to stand up for themselves."

– Hillary Clinton

Powerful people naturally take up space because they demand it. I have found that as women, we sometimes play ourselves too small when it comes to demanding respect, benefits, or positions that we rightfully deserve. Some of the skills which I believe many of us lack include the ability to design clear objectives for our lives, and developing the resilience to push forward in obtaining our heart's desires, no matter the resistance that we will face. For instance, now that men and women are given access to the same opportunities, I would imagine that both sexes would have the same growth trajectory. However, the reality that we see in the corporate environment shows us that men and women are still speaking different languages and working under different expectations.

A study conducted by Google in 2008 found that women within the organization were being promoted at a much lower rate than the men (Clarke, 2019). The study found that the reason behind fewer women representatives in higher roles boiled down to the process of how promotions took place. During that time in the organization, those who would be considered for a promotion had to raise their heads and approach their senior managers with a request for a promotion. As a result of this process, women were seen to be promoting themselves at a slower rate than men. Once this data was found, Google shared it with its entire organization, explaining the trend that was happening and urging women to promote themselves more—fortunately, they did.

It is a tough pill to swallow, knowing that you are standing in your own way and preventing yourself from succeeding. I find that it is always easier to identify the external hindrances to our success but ignore our own role in removing the barriers that we have created between us and our goals. I can imagine that there are many things that are restraining you from living a life which reflects your own ideas of peace and freedom. Some of the factors that are limiting you are out of your control and thus, you can do nothing about them. Nevertheless, there are some factors which are holding you back that you can *absolutely* control. These include factors that are related to your own self-perception and how you see the world around you. Exposing yourself to these factors and understanding the ways in which they can manifest in your life will give you the confidence of appropriately dealing with them and choosing to let them go.

The Lack of Self-Esteem and Self-Efficacy

Self-esteem refers to the opinion that you have of yourself. Thus, you can identify individuals with a high self-esteem by the value they ascribe to themselves and their achievements. It is natural for all of us to doubt our abilities sometimes, or fear failing at a task, however, individuals with a low self-esteem feel dissatisfied with themselves more often than not. Some of the other ways of identifying low self-esteem, perhaps even in your own life, would be seen in having a cynical opinion about your efforts, skills, or progress in your life. Along with being cynical about your abilities, you would also feel the need to downgrade or ignore the positive qualities within yourself. You would notice the feeling of inferiority to others, which would also cause you to become very judgmental about the efforts and skills of others. Furthermore, you would notice a pattern of negative self-talk in your mind and the thoughts of negative words or phrases repeatedly about yourself and others.

A low self-esteem will also affect the quality of your life. Besides the negative feelings that you experience internally, the quality of your relationships will also be impacted. For instance, a person with low self-esteem may find it difficult to create healthy boundaries with their colleagues or relatives and thus, they are more susceptible to being abused. This type of person may also find it difficult to express their grievance or pain, opting instead to accept poor treatment.

Those with a low self-esteem can also display signs of being perfectionists and applying severe pressure on themselves to over-achieve in order to make up for their perceived shortcomings. I also find that people with a low self-esteem struggle to become resilient when faced with trials or stress. Due to their negative self-talk feeding them lies about their hopelessness in a situation or crisis, they are less likely to be proactive in finding solutions on how to overcome or endure through present challenges.

A lack of self-esteem will invariably lead to a lack of self-efficacy. Self-efficacy, in simple terms, is the belief that you have in your own ability to succeed in a particular situation presented to you. In other words, if you undermine your own voice, skills, or talents, it becomes challenging to achieve success in any particular venture or task that will require you to take risks, be courageous, or create opportunities for yourself. This should show us that one of the prerequisites for attaining success is carrying a deep seated belief in your own abilities. For someone who has a low self-esteem, goals are seen as major risks that have potential to fail and cause more harm than good. Those with a low self-esteem are not prone to make any decision that would take them out of their comfort zone or allow them to experience another side of their reality. Thus, we can see that self-efficacy can significantly impact people's behaviors and the goals that they set and seek to accomplish.

Once you commit to a goal and find the conviction to see it through, you will find that you come across many stumbling blocks along your path to success. A person with high self-efficacy would notice these stumbling blocks and immediately start thinking of solutions to overcome them in order to get back on the path to attaining their goal. These people would perceive the challenge as being an opportunity to understand their mission more earnestly, and would know to adjust their strategies going forward. In other words, the stumbling block becomes a necessary tool or lesson for growth, and it creates a stronger sense of attachment or commitment with the goal at hand.

On the other side, a person with a low self-efficacy would perceive the stumbling block differently. First and foremost, they would create plans and strategies to try and minimize the likelihood of challenges on their path toward their goal. This is because when faced with challenges, people with low self-efficacy believe that they lack the resources needed to overcome these challenges. These stumbling blocks would be overwhelming for them because they do not believe in their own mental, emotional, or physical capabilities to resolve the conflict or sudden difficulties. Their loss of confidence in the face of trials is also owed to their innately negative self-image and the constant rehearsal of their personal failures in their minds.

Cultural and Social Barriers

Tatenda is a 22-year old young woman who lives in Nairobi, Kenya. When Tatenda graduated from high school she was told by her parents that her and her brother's future would look different from then onward. Her brother, who was a year older than her, was expected to pursue his educational career further and enroll at Kenyatta University. Tatenda's parents believed that their daughter's pursuit for a tertiary degree was a waste of time and money. Her future was already set in stone, predestined when she was still a young girl following after her mother's footsteps. Tatenda's responsibilities now were centered around preparing her for marriage and the rearing of children. Her daily activities would focus on making her the fittest wife, who would one day take care of her family and support her husband.

Tatenda's story is shared by many African women who are groomed from an early age to assume positions of dependency in a significantly patriarchal African society. Nonetheless, even in the West, we can find many stories of how women are coerced by patriarchal culture or social norms and practices that are dependent on the empowerment of men in order to sustain their livelihoods. As much as we have taken notable strides in uprooting gender inequality in our global community, there are still many barriers that have stifled our ability to take positive action in our lives. The gender gap creates barriers in the livelihoods of women by limiting or inhibiting our access to resources and other leadership and decision-making opportunities. In some extreme cases, violence is used as a measure to control and limit the access that we as women have to resources in our societies.

1. Biases

Social and cultural biases play a crucial role in closing doors for women in society. For instance, the pro-male bias places a higher value on the performance and contribution of men at work and at home than women. In the corporate environment, the pro-male bias has shown how male performance is lauded and overestimated above female performance, in particular, men are seen to be preferred across industries when it comes to hiring new employees, rewarding high performance, and when assessing competency. The pro-male bias was seen to be more pronounced in industries or job positions that were perceived to be more appropriate for men.

There is also a gender bias which we see when women in corporate positions decide to rear children. Choosing to become a mother comes with certain stereotypes about the level of competency that the woman has in accomplishing and excelling at her work. The assumption is that when women start bearing children, their commitment to their work will drop and they will be too preoccupied to perform and meet the demands of their jobs. A study that was conducted in the United Kingdom showed that close to half of working women were terrified of telling their seniors that they were expecting a child. This fear is not irrational because within the same study, it was found that 11% of working women are pushed out of their positions after coming back from maternity leave. This research shows us that there is a "motherhood penalty" that is enforced when women decide to have children, which significantly reduces their likelihood to be considered for promotions at work or salary increases.

2. Work Culture and Organization

Society does not apply the same expectations on men than they do on women when it comes to raising children, fulfilling domestic household duties, or looking after ageing parents or relatives. Even though much work has been done in acknowledging the invisible work that women perform without any compensation, there are still women across the world who spend two to ten times more time and money on unpaid care work than men. In some regions in the world, it is not rare to find women who are both the breadwinners and the caregivers in a household, while men are only expected to be breadwinners but not necessarily primary caregivers. This presents a double burden on women—not only are women expected to contribute financially to the economy of the home, but they are also expected to nurture and take care of the children, help them with their homework, nurse them when they are sick, and ensure that the house is cleaned and the clothes are washed.

Furthermore, sexism remains a major barrier of entry in certain career fields or job positions that women apply for. Such discrimination is more prevalent in male-dominated industries or organizations like film or engineering. When women enter these sexist industries or organizations, they are made to feel like an outsider, being less intelligent or less useful in the industry or organization than their male counterparts. Often these women cannot even share their experience at work with their colleagues because most of them are men who perpetuate this sexist attitude and behavior. Even the manager or senior authority who would typically resolve unfair disputes between co-workers is a man who cannot begin to relate to the reality of being disrespected and undermined for purely being a woman. Without any voice of reason or female representative in a senior position, many women either put up with the sexist behavior until they are so discouraged and disempowered at work that they eventually leave.

3. Women's Internal Barriers

Beyond the imposed cultural and social barriers, we must also face our own internal barriers too. It should not be a surprise to you that studies have shown women to have lower self-confidence than men, even when they are both educated and have similar ambitions in life. Women tend to speak less of their skills and talents than men and when faced with appraisals at work, women are more likely to give themselves lower scores than their male counterparts. We see ourselves as a work in progress and it shows in our reluctance to apply for better paying jobs or request for a salary increase at work. Even in our personal roles as mother, wife, or sister, we will place a lot of pressure on ourselves to be present and available to everyone all of the time. Our tendency is to compare our performance at being a mother, wife, or sister with that of another woman and critically judge to see whether our performance is weaker or at the same level.

Lastly, we are also burdened with the good girl syndrome, which is rooted from our cultural conditioning in our childhoods. Think back to when you were a young girl and try to remember the type of work or actions that you were rewarded for. I know in my own life, I remember being rewarded for being quiet, sitting with my legs closed, being polite to other people, and following directions without questioning the instructions. I didn't know at the time that my rewards were grooming me to become agreeable and avoid confrontations at all cost. This upbringing did not serve me when I entered the corporate environment; in fact, I believe that my good girl syndrome made me assume a more subservient attitude and made me always willing to sacrifice my comfort to appease others.

Communication Style

Women and men have different communication styles because of the nature of how communication styles are formed. Communication styles are created through our learned social behaviors, therefore, the fact the men and women are socialized differently means that the two will communicate in different ways. Nonetheless, both men and women need to learn how to communicate in a manner that inspires leadership and respect, in order to effectively make decisions that others will follow, or at least honor. The lack of clear communication can result in a loss of information and thus, lead to miscommunication or misunderstandings. For instance, when a woman is unclear in how she communicates with her co-workers, she may hinder the flow of communication throughout her department or team.

Men have a very unique way of communicating. They tend to be direct and straightforward in how they present information, keeping the message as linear as possible. They are typically concerned with either the punishment or solution rather than the reason behind the problem. Furthermore, most men display competitive qualities, especially in a corporate environment which includes a focus on their performance in comparison with others, becoming more authoritative in their roles, as well as focusing on the mission at hand and ways to achieve it as quickly as possible. For men, communication is a game of collecting and sharing information in order to get what they truly desire—the promise of a promotion.

Women communicate in a very different manner than men. Our communication style is generally indirect and polite, being considerate of how our perspective on reality can impact how the receiver interprets our message. Due to the indirect nature of our communication, it becomes difficult for us to present information in a linear and targeted fashion; instead we speak in circles, preferring to hint at the facts instead of addressing them directly. Women have also been conditioned over time to adopt "feminine" styles of communication. For instance, we have been told that it is woman-like to think and react to present circumstances with an emotional response. Thus, many women lead their lives, form relationships, and select jobs using cognitive flexibility, which refers to analyzing situations to figure out the "why" factor in order to develop several solutions.

However, as much as there are male or female communication styles, I find that many men and women do not always fit into these tightly woven boxes. Instead, I find that there are some men who display more feminine communication styles (what many would refer to as passive communication), and some women who display a more masculine communication style (what many would refer to as aggressive communication). Therefore, in seeking to empower women to become more confident in how they communicate at work and at home, I believe that it would be far more valuable to discuss which of the four popular communication styles would empower women to be seen and respected in both public and private spaces.

The Four Communication Styles

There are four broad communication styles that both men and women use to share information with others. These four communication styles include passive, passive-aggressive, aggressive, and assertive communication. When you understand how each communication style is displayed, you will be able to select one which will help you communicate and share your information, ideas, and feelings in a way that empowers you and the receiver. You will also find that the more you practice communicating effectively, the quality of your interactions will increase. Communicating with people requires a deep level of self-awareness and knowing what kind of behavior or message you are projecting.

I am sure you have had many conversations where your message was misinterpreted or you walked away feeling deflated from your words being misunderstood. The reason why some conversations leave us feeling light and positive and others leave us feeling discouraged, is due to the breakdown of communication between the two parties during a conversation. When you experience a communication breakdown, it is usually because you and the person you were speaking to had conflicting communication styles. Therefore, if you wanted to turn the situation around and improve on how you and the other person would engage in the future, you would need to learn which pattern or type of communication style they are displaying (while being mindful of your own communication style) and find ways of directing the conversation in a way that both of you can feel heard.

The first style of communication is passive communication. Passive communicators find it difficult to express their true thoughts and feelings outwardly to others. These types of communicators prefer to give in, or allow others to direct the conversation or decision-making outcome because of the fear of voicing their own opinions, which may or may not be perceived as being wrong or invalid. Due to the lack of openly sharing their messages with others, passive communicators end up feeling frustrated by the decisions that are made in a group or a team concerning them, which may not align with their own goals or desires. However, even this frustration is never released for others to see or resolve because of the fear of their frustration being seen as troublesome. Thus, passive communication typically leads to a build up of anger and resentment within the individual, without any outlet to genuinely share their thoughts and feelings.

The second style of communication is passive-aggressive communication. Passive-aggressive communicators do a great job of displaying a passive demeanor on the surface yet withholding a lot of built-up anger internally. Nonetheless, this aggressive nature does reveal itself in very subtle and indirect ways, which gives the receiver mixed signals about what message the passive-aggressive communicator is truly sharing. Some of the subtle ways which people show their passive-aggressive nature is through the two-toned messages that they will send simultaneously.

For instance, they may communicate using sarcasm or exaggerations, whereby the words that are coming out of their mouth do not align with their actions. Passive-aggressive communicators may also be dismissive when confronted and asked to clarify their message; they may respond with a dismissive "it's not important" or "I was only joking, relax!" The danger of this style of communication is seen in how passive-aggressive communicators cannot fully acknowledge the emotions that they are carrying and those expressed by others.

The third style of communication is aggressive communication. Aggressive communicators have a need to dominate every conversation and have the last word. For these types of communicators, communication is seen to be a win-lose game, whereby the aggressive communicator gets to share their message openly and the receiver must obey and passively agree to the ideas, thoughts, and opinions of the speaker. It is common to find an aggressive communicator dominating conversations both at home and at work; for them it is all about "me" and how influential their views and beliefs are in both public and private domains. The danger of using this style of communication is that it becomes difficult to allow other voices and opinions to be heard. Furthermore, aggressive communicators seek to command a conversation and thus, their deliverance may be interpreted as being rude, intimidating, crass, or threatening to those listening.

The fourth style of communication is assertive communication which is, according to me, the most effective way to deliver a message that will grab people's attention and encourage a positive response. Assertive communicators express their own perspectives on an issue or situation in a healthy way, being mindful of the needs of others and what they might be hearing. I prefer this style of communication because it encourages people to engage in an open dialogue where there are no winners or losers; both realities are respected and considered in how the parties share their message.

Assertive communication requires a confidence in believing that what you have to share is important, and therefore must be expressed. It also provides an opportunity for both parties to speak, which makes the conversation balanced and fruitful for all involved. Assertive communication will allow you to take ownership of your feelings and ideas instead of blaming them on others; for instance an assertive communicator would say "I feel undermined" rather than saying "you make me feel undermined."

It is clear to see how the first three communication styles could easily create misunderstandings. This is because they exclude the two most important ingredients of effective communication, which are honesty and vulnerability. When you are passive, you fear being vulnerable enough to share your genuine feelings with others. Those who are passive-aggressive find it difficult to be honest about the intention behind their words and messages. Aggressive communicators feel the need to dominate a conversation because they are fearful of losing control, which could expose their vulnerabilities and weaknesses. However, assertive communication allows for genuine interactions that are honest and open, allowing for issues to be raised and solutions to be found in a manner that empowers both parties.

Chapter Three:

Inspiration to Change

"Freeing yourself was one thing, claiming ownership of that freed self was another."

– Tony Morrison

There are many painful experiences that I have been through in my life that I believe would not have occurred if I was a man. I know that many of you who are reading this book have also experienced similar pain in your lives as a result of being undermined, harassed, and oppressed for merely being a woman. However, what I have found to be true in my life is that the only way to change how we experience the world is to first change how we look at it. Indeed, it is our own memories of having to endure suffering at the hands of sexist employers or abusive romantic partners that continue the perpetual cycle of suffering experienced in our current lives. In essence, our own mental programming continues, which sees the world through the eyes of the oppressed, and continues to stifle us even when our own freedom is within our reach.

Our freedom is not handed to us by the same employers or romantic partners who took advantage of us. Rather, this freedom is received internally by our willingness to demand change in our lives. There is only so much suffering anyone can bear before the desire for peace and freedom creeps into our minds and becomes more desirable than our current life experience. In other words, breaking out of old systems of oppressive thinking will require you to demand change. Perhaps you demand change in your career in the form of receiving better pay or finally being promoted to a higher position. Or maybe you demand change in how household chores and responsibilities are distributed between you, your spouse, and your children.

I can sincerely tell you that change is possible when it is desired more than the old systems and relationships that kept you imprisoned and dependent on other people, jobs, or governmental aid. The most notable way to manifest this change is to find inspiration which will guide you toward a more positive vision. For instance, if you were to demand change at work, you may choose to be inspired by other women who have worked their way up the corporate ladder and became company directors, CEO's, and board members. Focusing on this inspiring vision will allow you to remain committed to change and begin to live a life that makes room for a positive transformation to start occurring. No longer will your passive or submissive behavior help you at work, because your inspiration demands a more assertive attitude in communicating your needs and expectations in a healthy manner.

The Benefits of Becoming More Confident and Assertive

There is nothing that is impossible for you to do or to be. The perceived limits that you identify are only an indication of where you made a decision to stop and go no further. The sooner you realize that your breakthrough comes from releasing the limits that you have created, you will be empowered to seek positive change. One of the results of unleashing yourself from your own mental boundaries, is that you will become more confident and assertive in all that you do. In other words, confidence and assertiveness are byproducts of a liberated mind that is willing to see the possibilities in every circumstance. I find that this process does not work in reverse, meaning that you cannot first become confident and thereafter liberate your mind. Your mind must be the first to consent to seeing the power that you have to change your life, thereafter it becomes easier to adopt more positive and healthy behaviors and attitudes.

There are many benefits to becoming more confident and assertive in your life. In general, confidence and assertiveness will help you express yourself, which subsequently allows you to express your plans, ideas, decisions, grievances, or thoughts. The freedom of expression is a superpower on its own. When you feel comfortable to express who you are and what you need, you are able to progress in life because there are no barriers that you won't boldly challenge. You begin to feel powerful because for the first time, you are able to stand up for yourself and courageously say "no" if you have to. Confidence and assertiveness also communicate that you value yourself and therefore your words, and ideas deserve to be valued and respected; people will begin to treat you with the same high regard you offer to yourself. The following are benefits that you can also expect when you commit to being more confident and assertive.

The first benefit is that you will be able to feel in control of your own life. Confidence allows you to take positive action which will improve upon the way you live and experience your reality. You will feel a sense of responsibility to make your life as meaningful as you can, taking advantage of every opportunity that is presented to you. Secondly, confidence and assertiveness will allow you to communicate in more effective ways and share your thoughts and feelings without them being misunderstood. I find that the more confidence a person has, the healthier and stronger their relationship is with others. This is because communication is more open and embraces all perspectives of a situation, thus making others feel respected and heard.

The third benefit that you can expect to experience when you become more confident, is that you will start to accomplish more goals in your personal life. There are so many dreams that we keep hidden in our hearts, too afraid to express or entertain them. When we practice confidence and assertiveness, those dreams are pulled down from fantasy to reality through our initiatives, strategies, and plans to materialize them. Our goals also become more realistic because now that we are confident, we see that there is no limit to what we can achieve; we have a new found trust in our own action to lead us on the path to success. The fourth benefit to being confident and assertive is that others will assume that you are more intelligent than you truly are. Confident people display a strength and conviction that those who aren't confident do not have. It allows others to assume that you are more qualified at your job, have better leadership capabilities, and can be trusted with greater responsibilities.

Confidence and assertiveness can prove to be extremely useful in the workplace. This is because confident people are able to engage in authentic communication. They do not seek to hide their intentions like the passive-aggressive type, rather, they are secure in their own views and opinions enough that they do not fear sharing their thoughts with other coworkers or even those in senior positions. Confidence will allow you to speak with your managers with clarity and boldness, understanding that both of you have value to offer each other. You will begin to see opportunities to engage with others as win-win scenarios where all parties will walk away feeling understood and embraced. There are a few steps that you can take to begin perceiving all opportunities of networking with others as being a win-win scenario.

The first step is to write down or think about what assertiveness means to you. Think about what it would look like if you became assertive or some great examples of assertive behavior that you have witnessed before. The second step is to assess the relationships that you have with others in your life (both professional and personal relationships) and consider those relationships which do not empower you to become assertive. Perhaps these relationships weigh you down or highlight your insecurities in some way. After reflecting on these disempowering relationships, decide to distance yourself from them, or if it is within a company, consider moving departments in order to free yourself from the constant exposure to negativity.

The third step is to refrain from believing that every thought that is processed in your mind is correct. Instead, create a quick system that can qualify each thought, keeping those which are positive and useful and discarding those which are self-defeating. For instance, you can decide to pay attention to your self-talk and assess the negative opinions or judgements that you hear yourself rehearsing in your mind. Once you have identified the negative self-talk, ask yourself whether this idea or thought is aligned to the plans and ideas you have about your life. If they are not, choose to discard them by replacing the negative thought or judgement with a positive affirmation or idea.

The fourth step is to quit apologizing and start owning your mistakes. You don't have to apologize after every small error because it is human nature to make small errors. Instead, it would be more empowering for you to learn from every small error and let your changed behavior be the apology. Confident people own their mistakes without making themselves feel bad for making the mistake in the first place. Therefore, it is better to take responsibility for your mistakes and never dwell on the mistake for too long—you are allowed to make mistakes without feeling guilty. The fifth and final step is to welcome and respect feedback. Feedback should not be seen as a personal attack or a way to diminish your efforts, instead, you should view feedback as an opportunity to adjust your delivery or processes in order to become more successful at a task. Make it a habit to consistently ask your senior manager for feedback on your work or performance in order to gage the effectiveness of your ideas, plans, and strategies at work.

The Virtuous Cycle

It is a common belief within the corporate environment that happiness is only attainable once you have reached a certain level of success. However, research is showing us that the process works in the reverse; that being happy at work is the multiplier of your success. The amount of influence that you can have on other people works in the same manner; for instance, you do not need to have money or reach a certain level of success before you can have influence in your community. Rather, being useful in your community will offer you many opportunities of making money and becoming successful. Therefore, what becomes evident is that our ability to be effective and achieve our full potential lies in the positive feedback loop that we create.

The positive feedback loop, also known as a virtuous cycle, creates compounding success from the momentum of one positive initiative which led to a positive effect. The opposite of a virtuous cycle is what is called a vicious cycle where negative thoughts or actions cascade and create a momentum or loop of negative consequences. For instance, if you do not enjoy the kind of work that you do, you will eventually become disengaged or complacent, which will lead to poor results or outcomes that will make you feel even more discouraged about your work. The virtuous cycle on the other hand, creates an upward spiral, leading you to your goals one positive decision at a time. In other words, with every victory that you achieve, you are given access to more opportunities to achieve greater victories. Very soon, attaining successful outcomes becomes easier and easier, making it look natural and requiring little effort.

Part of the reason why the virtuous cycle leads to success is because it calls for collaboration or collective effort. Even if you begin your journey alone, there will always be a phase which will require that you ask for assistance from those with more power or authority than you. In essence, your positive actions lead you to work or engage with successful people who can empower you with resources that can take you to the next level. The virtuous cycle can also be used to motivate an organization or team to collectively aim for the greater good. For instance, a manager can decide to reward her team for achieving impressive results, and this act of goodness can lead to the team working more diligently to achieve greater results than before. Therefore, virtuous cycles extend opportunities of change and goodness to many people, causing them to work together to achieve a collective dream or goal.

You can also practice using the virtuous cycle in your own life. This process of compounding positivity and success will help you create a positive momentum, which will bring many opportunities, positive ideas, and plans in your life. The first step to creating a virtuous cycle would be to participate in an activity or action outside of your comfort zone. This can feel uncomfortable at first, but remember that it feels uncomfortable because it is new and not necessarily because it is bad for you. Try those activities that you have always dreaded doing like singing at a karaoke bar, posting a selfie on your social media, or learning how to make a new recipe. The point of the first step is to challenge you to see that there is more to your life than your present experiences.

The second step is to realize that no matter how disastrous you may have been in performing your first step, your world didn't come shattering down and you didn't lose your dignity or sanity. In fact, you may realize that by performing the first step, you gained a new skill or experienced a new feeling. Perhaps you realized that you are able to have fun in other ways which did not seem accessible to you before. The third step is to attempt the first step again, however, this time, put a little more effort. Since you will be repeating the same activity or exercise that you did in the first step, you will be more comfortable doing it and it will feel like less of a threat or a risk than before. On this occasion, focus on enjoying the activity, paying attention to how it makes you feel and relaxing any tension in your body while performing it.

The fourth step is to assess what is working and what isn't. In this step you will review the activity that you performed in step one and three and find ways that could make performing this activity more enjoyable, organized, fulfilling, or meaningful. For instance, if you decided to prepare a new recipe, you could find ways to improve upon the recipe through adding more flavor or serving it at a different setting with different people. Once you have identified ways of heightening your experience, do the activity again with the new adjustments made. Step five involves seeking advice from an expert who has mastered the activity that you are now becoming qualified at performing.

An experienced expert can provide mentorship through giving you feedback on how to perform the activity to the best of your abilities. They will be able to teach you new skills, and tips on how to improve upon your techniques. This will significantly help you skip many years of trial and error and increase your confidence in performing this activity in the future. The more you continue to engage with these five steps, the greater you will become in performing an activity, and soon you will be an expert in it. Imagine how many skills or talents you can learn and master by creating a virtuous cycle of learning a skill and improving it. The more experience you gain in an activity, the greater your confidence will be in performing it, and thus, you will continue to perpetuate a positive momentum of success actions.

Real Life Stories of How Confidence and Assertiveness Can Change Your Life

Your commitment to regaining control over your life and moving forward with a fearless confidence will propel you in your success. The encouraging part about reclaiming your confidence is that you are not the first woman to travel this path of self-discovery and healing from past painful ordeals. There have been many women throughout history who have succeeded against all odds stacked against them. While there are a few popular stories of famous women who have cheated death or survived extreme forms of torture and suffering, there are so many unsung heroines who are not celebrities, yet they too, have endured great suffering and have overcome through great conviction in who they are and deciding to never quit until their lives reflected the quality of their hopes and dreams. I would like to share with you some of their stories to empower you to take the necessary action in changing your life for the better.

The Story of Callie Davis

My name is Callie Davis. I am a 32-year-old woman living in rural Ireland with my boyfriend Peter and our furry cat Pixie. I started having self-esteem issues early on in my school years—my earliest memories are from secondary school. I was never the girl who had straight hair or an athletic body, in fact, I never felt like I fit in with any particular group of friends. As a result of my awkwardness, I was bullied, however, it was more mental than physical bullying.

Some of the bullying I remember was being laughed at, being picked on by mean girls, and having boys reject my advances. During my teen years, I guess I had internalized all of the negative words that were spoken to me throughout secondary school to the extent that it caused a lot of grief. I suffered from depression and I started hating myself; how I looked, the awkward interests I had, and how I was afraid to show others who I really was. Wearing figurative masks to hide the real me throughout high school and in my twenties made me fall in love with troubled men. For some reason, I felt that I could relate with their insecurities and I could—in some way—fix them and make them whole.

I accepted poor treatment from men and with each relationship, my self-esteem deteriorated more and more. I was never truly in love with any of my exes, however, letting them go would make me feel unlovable and hollow inside. I needed them to validate that at least one person in the world loved me enough to date me. I suffered much emotional abuse and after a while, it always became physical. When I think about how tired and hopeless I felt in my relationships, I cannot help but cry. I was depending on another human being to affirm me at the expense of my own dignity and self-respect. However, everything changed when I came across a community mental health program offering free counselling for a limited time only.

The program changed my life. It is where I first discovered what it meant to have self-love. All of this time, I had thought that self-love was putting on a face of confidence, but I learned that self-love was found through embodying confidence. It was less about acting like I believed in myself, and instead about taking time to learn the many reasons why I was so special and all of my abilities that made me useful in my community. I started focusing more on my strengths and using them to catapult me forward in life. Through maximizing my strengths, I came to work as a waitress for an old bakery in a nearby town. I had always loved baking since I was a little girl, and now I found myself surrounded by delicious baked goods every day.

Through sharing my interests with my colleagues and allowing them to get to know me, I was offered an opportunity to apply to become one of the pastry chefs at the store. I took the offer and after a grueling application process, I was the only one chosen out of 10 other qualified and experienced pastry chefs. This promotion gave me the confidence to take my craft more seriously and within three years, I had become a qualified pastry chef. I see so many possibilities in my life now and I know that my journey is not over yet. There are still so many dreams I have to fulfill in order to make my younger, awkward self proud.

The Story of Diana Williamson

My name is Diana Williamson and I am a 25-year-old young lady born and raised in Bakersfield, California. As a little girl I would say that I was fairly confident; I was comfortable playing with barbie dolls and kicking a ball on the field without feeling boxed by my gender. My self-esteem problems began in high school, when I changed schools and I started noticing that I was much different than the other girls. I was 5 feet 8 inches tall and weighed 240 pounds. Before then, I never really noticed that I was overweight. I guess my parents and community did a great job at sheltering me. The high school boys however, were not as accommodating to my "weird" body.

Naturally, I started to observe who the boys would give their attention to. I found that it was always the young girl who was 5 feet 2 inches tall and weighed 100 pounds. Her hair was always beautifully draped on her shoulders and her face had no blemishes at all. I started to keep a low profile, fearing more ridicule and harassment if I was seen too often. I behaved like a shy girl even though I was far from it, because I never wanted people to comment on my appearance. The last time anyone heard a word coming out of my mouth was when I confessed to being attracted to a fairly thin boy who was shorter than I was. You can imagine how much ridiculing and talk my confession created. I was advised by some students to only approach boys who were like me, "tall and fat," because I would not be anyone else's type.

I managed to remain invisible throughout high school, however, when I went to college, I wanted to change the narrative about who I was. Not only did I want to lose weight for my own comfort, I wanted to also change how I saw myself internally. I learned very quickly in college that girls with a thinner frame are plagued with insecurities too; some of them feel less of a woman with small breasts and others feel less of a woman with narrow hips. Therefore, I realized that weight loss was not the end all and be all of my struggles. My self-perception needed a transformation as urgently as my body did. I lost 70 pounds over two years but that wasn't the best part of my transformation.

I decided to use my own experience with body shaming to start a student support group where we would offer support to those struggling with body issues. I wanted to lend my voice to those who may have been going through the hell I went through in high school and let them know that I see them. I became comfortable speaking about my experience being overweight and I saw how much it made other young women and men open up about their struggles with being overweight too. Now I am able to accept a compliment and genuinely believe it instead of thinking it was said out of pity. My weight loss journey is still on track and I cannot wait to see the impact that my story has on many other young women like myself.

The Story of Hannah Mason

My name is Hannah Mason and I am a 42-year-old woman living in South Carolina. I grew up in a family where both of my parents suffered from mental illnesses. My mother was diagnosed with depression when I was only five and my father was an alcoholic who went in and out of rehab until his tragic passing a few weeks after my 22nd birthday. Being an only child in a dysfunctional family led to me adopting negative ways of thinking about myself and where I would end up in life. I never encouraged myself to participate in school or take on extracurricular activities. As a consequence of this, I missed out on many educational opportunities available to me at the time.

My self-confidence was deeply wounded after high school when I could not attend college due to my sub-par performance at school and having parents who were emotionally unavailable. The lack of support and reassurance that I was a brilliant kid and had a bright future led me in the arms of older men. I was looking for a father figure; someone to give me the nurturing that I did not receive as a young girl. However, I was subject to emotional abuse and an oppressive life away from home. When I was 25, I managed to escape from a toxic relationship with my then fiancé, carrying my two-year-old son on my back.

My son and I stayed in relatives' homes until I found a decent administrative job that could pay me enough money for us to live alone. It was during the many sleepless nights spent watching my little boy doze off that I decided that it was time for me to make a change. I started to imagine myself owning my own home and having enough room for a pool where my son could spend his summer days. I began to take my role at work seriously, and at times I would request more work to do. Very quickly, I started acquainting myself with my senior managers who were always enthusiastic to hand over more work. It was the speed at which I worked that impressed them and eventually, I found myself invited to training sessions that taught me how to perform more advanced tasks.

Within two years of making a decision to change my life for the better, I had been promoted to a new position as team leader of my unit. Not only did my salary increase by 5 times the amount I earned starting out, I was also eligible to take out a bond and purchase my first home. This was a very empowering time in my life because for the first time, I believed that I was truly capable. I saw how powerful I was when I committed to a plan and took action. My self-confidence grew greater when I started to take on more responsibility in my life and become more valuable to others. Every day I practice gratitude and count my past as one of my greatest blessings because without it, I would have never known how courageous I can be in the face of crisis.

Part Two:

Build Your Confidence

Chapter Four:

Make a Mind Shift to Build Your

Inner Confidence

"If you're one of those people who has that little voice in the back of her mind saying, 'Maybe I could do [fill in the blank],' don't tell it to be quiet. Give it a little room to grow, and try to find an environment it can grow in."

– Reese Witherspoon

Have you ever been through a challenging time in your life and once the trial was over, you felt it was all for nothing? I find that at times, adversity comes into our lives, wreaks havoc, and then leaves without mending all of the broken pieces of our heart. There is always a part of us however, that continues to search for the light in a dark situation, in order to make sense of what happened to us or what we experienced. We want to be able to say that we learned valuable lessons from the difficulties that we endured and, in some way, make up for lost time.

When I was much younger, I used to believe that experiencing adversity was a necessary process that would lead to my happiness. I thought that happiness was the reward at the end of a road of much suffering; a sort of incentive for enduring tough times. My mentality towards happiness was not proactive at all. Instead, I left it to chance and hoped that my life circumstances would change eventually. It didn't matter how much I fantasized about one day being free from my oppressive job or finally living a life that didn't bring me so much pain, the truth was I wasn't taking any actions toward realizing this life. Happiness was a dream that I would entertain in my thoughts but never practically reach for in my waking life.

I came to a point where enough was enough. What once was a pleasant dream started to haunt me. I wanted to be happy so much that I could no longer wait for it to find me—I was ready to finally search for happiness on my own. Along my journey of seeking, I realized that if I wanted to experience happiness, I had to find a way of changing the narrative that I had created about my life for the past ten years. By changing my perspective of the suffering that I had endured at the time, I would lessen the pain that I was experiencing every day. Therefore, I decided to reflect on my life and reflect back on some of the difficult times that I had experienced at work and in my family home growing up. As I recalled each memory, I challenged myself to replace the narrative that I had created with a more empowering one which made me a heroine instead of a victim.

For instance, I considered the painful memory of having to leave my job because of the abuse I faced at the hands of co-workers and I made a new narrative. The new narrative saw the abuse that I faced at work as being a necessary wake up call to show me that I had a low self-esteem and that I needed to create healthier boundaries. The act of leaving my job was also a necessary part of my growth because it marked the beginning of a life spent living on my own terms; and ultimately leading to me writing this book. Without having gone through this experience, I would not be where I am today. Therefore, I found that it takes shifting your mindset and accepting both the good and the bad from your past to find the peace and happiness that you are looking for today.

Once my mentality shifted, I found that I could learn a number of lessons from going through adversity. Firstly, I learned that adversity is temporary. Every crisis or difficulty that you will face in your life has an expiry date. You may not know when it will be over, however, I can assure you that it has an end. Shifting your mindset and believing that your suffering will not last forever, will immediately lessen the burden you are carrying. Eventually, you will start to gain confidence during the present difficulty and it will lose its power over you for good. Secondly, I learned that adversity is an anchor. The adversity that I overcame humbled me. It made me assess what truly mattered most in my life and those things that were distractions. Before changing my perspective on my past, my adversity was an anchor weighing me down; I felt defeated every time I would think negatively about my life and situation. However, I was set free from this anchor when I decided to see it differently.

Furthermore, I learned that adversity was my greatest teacher and without it, I wouldn't know how to become the best version of myself. I was challenged by my hardship to the extent that I had no choice but to grow up and see my life differently. Adversity can also become your greatest teacher if you reframe your negative experiences and allow the wisdom in your pain to emerge. Finally, adversity taught me that every situation—regardless of how terrible it looks or feels—carries with it a seed of goodness. Not everybody will find this seed of goodness because not everybody is looking for it. Our perspective on our lives truly matters because we will only live within the parameters of our visions and our thoughts. When we choose to see pain, we will inevitably live in a vicious cycle of pain, however, when we strain our eyes to see even a glimpse of goodness or value, we will break free from the vicious cycle and enter a virtuous cycle of goodness.

Create a Better Mindset

The solution for turning our lives around for the better is found in creating a better mindset. It is true that none of us can avoid pain or live a life with constant highs. I guarantee you that at some point in your life, you will be challenged with grief, suffering, or any other form of pain which can disorientate you. How you choose to deal with the pain that you are faced with will determine the quality of your life going forward. You may not have been in control of the sudden pain that hit you, however, you are in control of the meaning and purpose that you ascribe to the pain.

In your life, you are the highest authority, carrying complete responsibility regarding which direction your life takes and how much growth you experience along the journey. Assuming that you want to travel on a successful path (despite the difficulty that you have experienced in your life) it would be necessary for you to adopt a mindset of positive thinking. Thinking positively is not an easy process for a person who has made a habit out of thinking negatively. It would require them to change some of their beliefs and replace self-defeating ones with empowering ones. It takes a lot of courage to decide to let go of the judgements, criticism, disappointment, and bitter memories that we have stored in our minds for many years. Thus, positive thinking is more of a lifestyle change than a mere practice of goodwill; it will require continuous practice and the intense monitoring of your thoughts.

Your thoughts are at the center of your mindset. Positive thoughts create an empowered mind and negative thoughts create a defeated mind. Moreover, your thoughts also have the power to determine your attitude. For instance, positive thoughts create a confident and assertive attitude, yet negative thoughts create a cynical and aggressive attitude. Your positive thoughts are also not limited to how you see yourself. Instead, your commitment to positive thinking will transform how you see others, as well as adjust how you experience the world around you. Your frame of reference and narrative about your current reality will become more encouraging, and you will see the good even in a bad situation. In other words, your commitment to positive thinking will allow you to live in a state of possibilities amidst difficult times. Seeing possibilities will, in essence, create a virtuous cycle that will lead to many opportunities for success.

There are so many benefits to positive thinking that I could possibly not count all of them. Nonetheless, there are a few that stand out to me. Firstly, positive thinking allows you to have a positive attitude. The reason why having a positive attitude is so advantageous, is due to the fact that a positive attitude removes the victim mentality. Instead of thinking that life is happening *to* you and that you have no control over your circumstances, a positive attitude will empower you to believe that life is happening *for* you, and that every circumstance you face is a stepping stone to manifesting the best version of yourself. People with a positive attitude tend to attract others who have the same joyful spirit. Even at work, people with a positive attitude are more likeable and approachable, due to their warm and friendly demeanor.

Secondly, positive thinking has the ability to reduce stress in your life because you are no longer carrying as much tension in your mind and body. In other words, the process of changing your response to stressful situations can effectively reduce the fight-or-flight response in your body. If you are swarmed with piles of tasks at work, positive thinking will encourage you to set reasonable deadlines or request for help if you are unable to complete it on your own. Thinking positively about your workload will allow you to communicate when you feel overwhelmed, making you feel supported and thus, stress-free.

Positive thinking also brings good health. The positive effects on your mind are further experienced in your body through a healthy digestive and immune system. People who make it a habit to think positively are less prone to illnesses because of their mental and physical strength. A positive thinker's body is present and able to fight off unwanted negative thoughts, emotions, and sickness, which come to invade their body. Positive thinkers are also less likely to suffer from mental illnesses such as depression or anxiety, due to their healthy process of dealing with pressure, grief, or loss. Furthermore, positive thinking allows you the opportunity to form healthy and prosperous relationships with others. Positive people will always leave a lasting impression in every conversation that they have with other people. There is just something so special about them that inspires others to get to know them better. Everyone is drawn to a positive person because they have the power to make others feel good about themselves.

There are a few practices that you can adopt today which will help you adjust your mentality and think more positively. The first one is practicing meditation. Meditation is the spiritual practice of being still and allowing your mind to come to a place of quietness naturally. In this place of mental quietness, you are able to let go of the mental dialogue and simply experience the moment as it is. Regular practice of meditation will clear up stored negative emotions and release them from your body. This is done through letting go of the attachments to your old patterns of thinking. Meditation will also allow you to see things for how they are now in each moment, giving you a fresh perspective on life and a more positive outlook. Another practice that you can adopt today is the practice of mindfulness.

Mindfulness is the practice of bringing your full awareness to the present moment. In order to do this, you would need to take time to be still (perhaps during a moment of meditation) and release your thoughts from your past and your future. In other words, let go of thinking about what could have happened or what will happen tomorrow, and bring your awareness to what is happening now. Mindfulness will empower you to take positive action now, instead of waiting for a favorable time in the future. It will also allow you to come to a place of forgiveness and making peace with your past, because in the awareness of the present moment, you will find that there is no more pain or suffering inside of you—the pain is attached to memories, negative habits, and behaviors, which have followed you from your past.

Finally, you can become a positive thinker by practicing gratitude regularly. Gratitude is the awareness that you have all that you will ever need in each moment. Instead of comparing what you have with what you used to have or what you hope to have in the future, gratitude allows you to find the peace in what is already here. There are so many blessings that you can count in your life right now, and bringing your awareness to them will make you more positive about your life. It can be as simple as being grateful for having three meals a day, not having to worry about where you are going to live, how you are going to stay warm; or alternatively, it can be as abstract as being grateful for your resilience in overcoming difficult times.

Develop Mental Toughness

Have you ever wondered what makes athletes commit to rigorous training, how working mothers are able to get home early enough to cook and do homework with their children, or how leaders are able to lead an organization of thousands of employees successfully? The common conclusion that most of us come to when we consider how people are able to live disciplined and highly successful lives, is that they must be extremely talented or have mastered some type of skill. We say to ourselves "she's been training since she was a kid," or "she's a manager so her work hours are not as intense as others." I am convinced that in our minds, we know that there must be more to the story than our quick judgements.

Research has found that our talents or skills don't play as much of a significant role in our success as we may think. In fact, it was found that our human intelligence only makes up 30% of our achievements. What was found to be of greater importance and a predictor of success was mental toughness. Studies looking into mental toughness continue to find that this superpower plays a greater role than any other factor in achieving our goals in business, relationships, and health. This is good news to those who feel as though they are not smart enough to accomplish anything noble in life. The playing field has now been leveled, and anyone who displays mental toughness can become prosperous in life.

An example of mental toughness is seen in how new cadets are recruited in the U.S. military. Every year, it is estimated that 1,300 cadets will join the United States Military Academy, West Point, as beginners. During their first summer initiation on campus, cadets will be required to complete some of the most grueling tests. Many insiders refer to this summer initiation program as "Beast Barracks." The purpose of Beast Barracks is to assess the mental, physical, and emotional capacity of each cadet. Therefore, those who end up succeeding this brutal testing are seen to be the most qualified to represent the military for their strength and intelligence.

Nonetheless, a researcher from the University of Pennsylvania, Angela Duckworth, wanted to see what exactly made cadets endure the testing of the Beast Barracks (Clear, 2013). She followed 2,441 cadets across two beginning classes at the Academy and measured each cadet's high school ranking, SAT score, Leadership Potential Score, Physical Aptitude Test score, as well as a Grit score (which measures each cadet's perseverance and commitment to long-term goals). At the end of her test, Angela found that it wasn't physical strength or the leadership score of the cadet that was the predictor of their success, rather, she found that it was the Grit score that made a remarkable difference. In fact, her research found that cadets that were a standard deviation higher in Grit, were 60% more likely to endure the Beast Barracks test than their peers. In other words, it was the mental toughness of the cadet that would determine their success, instead of genetics or previous experience.

I am sure that you have seen evidence of mental toughness overriding intelligence in your own life. Have you never seen a friend or relative who was so talented, yet nothing became of it? Or a co-worker who entered the company having no degree but over time, managed to climb the corporate ladder and occupy a high-paying position? It happens all around us, yet we have never fully grasped how these people do it. Evidence of mental toughness being the predictor of our success, shows us that our goals are, in fact, achievable, with or without access to resources when we start. It is not *what* we have that gives us an advantage in achieving our goals, but instead it is in our staying power. Staying power is our ability to endure through a task until it is complete or a desired result has been fulfilled. When we have built staying power, the challenges that we face along our road to success will not deter us from moving forward. Even when our progress has been stalled by unforeseen circumstances, we will find other alternatives of accomplishing the goals that we have set out to do.

During LaRae Quy's four month training program at the FBI Academy in Quantico, she was plunged into a culture that valued physical strength. Being a woman, her abilities were questioned and her ambition to work for the FBI seemed inappropriate. Even though LaRae had scored highly on her cognitive and personality tests, the mere fact that she was a woman made her seem inadequate or too weak to qualify for the program. Nonetheless, she continued to persevere through the program and refused to let how her peers perceived her to become a source of discouragement. She decided to change her perspective on the criticism that she continuously received, and see it as being an opportunity to prove that she was more than capable to succeed in this intense environment.

LaRae displayed mental toughness in the face of adversity, and her determination to break through barriers that were discriminatory against women led to her successfully completing the program and becoming an FBI agent. Not only was LaRae Quy an FBI agent, she went on to become a valuable member of the organization. She served as an agent for 24 years and during her time in service, she was known to expose foreign spies and recruit them to work for the American government. LaRae Quy's story is recorded in history due to her mental resilience in an environment full of risk, uncertainty, and a lot of deception. Her display of mental toughness became what set her apart from other agents and made her successful in her work.

Take Risks

The story of LaRae Quy shows us that sometimes, going out of our comfort zone can be advantageous for our personal and career growth. In fact, if you consider all of the people who have gone on to accomplish amazing feats in the world, you will see that they were bold enough to travel uncharted terrains or make risky decisions. Going out of your comfort zone looks different for every individual. For one person, it may be learning to speak up during a team meeting, and for another person, it can be going on dates frequently in order to find your true love.

I believe that many of us would travel out of our comfort zones more often if doing so did not cause so much uncertainty. Indeed, part of taking risks means that we need to be comfortable with uncertainty. Uncertainty makes us feel uneasy and makes us doubt whether we will successfully accomplish the goal at hand. It is common to be burdened with many fears when you are doing something different; usually, you will feel a deep fear of failure or rejection. Your inner voice will propose many "what if" scenarios such as "what if no one claps for me?" "what if my date is not attracted to me?" or "what if my business venture fails?"

We tend to place our focus on the outcome of our act of courage instead of focusing on the process itself. Inevitably, when we try to calculate the end without first taking the steps to get there, we will have many fears presented to us. However, when we start taking steps forward and exploring the many paths presented to us on the way, our fears begin to dissolve and suddenly, we are confident in our ability to take another step forward. What I am trying to say is, risk is only fearful when you have not taken any action. For instance, going on a date is terrifying when you haven't found a potential date, scheduled a meet up, and taken the time to go on the date and get to know them. The view from the outside looking in is always different than the view from the inside. Risk becomes less of a barrier when we decide to take one step forward, followed by another.

There are two common qualities found in all risk-takers, and they are the acceptance of failure and overconfidence. Risk-takers are not fearful of failing, rather, they see failure as a necessary tool to build their character. The process of achieving a goal changes you as an individual because your limits are stretched beyond the points that you had established previously. During this process, you may face disappointment or rejection. These seemingly undesirable emotions can help you develop mental toughness or build resilience. Failure does not need to be a dead end anymore. It can be seen to be a necessary pit stop that increases our staying power. Secondly, risk-takers are overconfident, which ultimately helps them to cope with failure.

There are many hurdles that entrepreneurs face when developing their businesses and most of the time, they are forced to take significant risks without knowing the outcomes of their decisions. Confidence allows them to trust in their own abilities and intuition to make strategic decisions and act swiftly. However, not all entrepreneurs are born confident; confidence is a skill that many of them must learn and practice in order to become good at it. This means that with practice, you can also learn how to confidently take risks and live beyond the parameters you have set in your own life.

One of the ways in which you can learn how to become a risk-taker is by changing how your brain is wired. It is a myth that once we reach adulthood, our brains are hard-wired and it is impossible to learn new habits or remove old ones. Research has found that our brains are more malleable than what we may think, and because of this, it is possible to shift our mentality. In our youth, changes to our brain are easily performed because our brain grows and changes naturally; however, in our adulthood, we need to play a greater role in influencing the formation of new habits and thought patterns.

Neuroplasticity is the brain's way of changing its makeup constantly through the creation of new neural pathways and getting rid of pathways that are no longer useful. In your adulthood, you can influence the adoption of new habits and beliefs by encouraging your brain's neuroplasticity. When you keep your brain flexible, you are able to continue learning throughout your adult years, grow in emotional intelligence, and keep your brain open-minded in order to overcome biases in your adult life. Encouraging your neuroplasticity is not as simple as playing a game of chess or sudoku; in order to rewire itself, your brain will require constant practice of a new activity or constant affirmation of a belief system.

Moreover, you can influence your neuroplasticity by altering your responses to common situations in your life. For instance, if your brain is wired to avoid meeting and getting to know new people due to the fear of rejection, you can place your brain outside of its comfort zone by making it a habit to strike a conversation with strangers that you meet in the grocery store or shopping mall. Practicing performing a new skill will keep your brain flexible and help it become more resilient in switching tasks and adopting new habits. Lastly, you can influence your brain's neuroplasticity by adopting a growth mindset.

A person with a growth mindset sees constant room for transformation in their lives. While those with a fixed mindset avoid challenges at all costs, people who have a growth mindset seek new challenges all of the time, in order to find new ways to grow. They look at life as one big learning experience and find value in the journey, instead of desiring to reach the destination. As we get older, we may be discouraged to learn new skills or develop our character, because we believe that our years of youthful expression or zeal for life are nearing an end. This belief is not true at all. Regardless of the phase in life that we are in, there are always opportunities to be seized. All of these opportunities lie beyond our comfort zones. Therefore, instead of reminiscing about the good old days or allowing your fear of criticism, humiliation, rejection, or failure stop you, take advantage of the time you have to learn a new skill, hobby, or take on a new risk—you will find a new life waiting for you to experience!

Reader Task: Keeping a Thought Diary

In this chapter, we spoke about the many ways of shifting our mindset to embrace change. One of the best ways to shift our mindset is through changing the quality of our thoughts. Our thought life has a powerful impact on how we choose to experience our lives, and our state of happiness and peace in our current life situation. Negative thoughts carry a negative influence in how we see ourselves and our power to overcome adversity. It is therefore important for us to track our negative thoughts through the use of a thought diary, in order to identify negative thoughts before they start chipping away at our self-confidence.

When you are presented with a situation where you feel as though you are at risk or in danger, you can activate your negative beliefs. When your negative beliefs are activated, you will find that your thoughts become harsh and critical of your performance. You will start placing harmful labels on yourself, undermine your efforts, and in some cases, chastise yourself physically. During moments of being highly critical of yourself, you are likely to withdraw yourself from others, try to overcompensate for your perceived lack of intelligence or skills, or avoid opportunities of growth or responsibility presented to you. Eventually, the negative thoughts lead to a downward spiral of negative events which can cause mental illness.

A thought diary can help you challenge your negative thoughts by allowing them to be exposed. This does not need to be done in a self-critical manner, instead you can see it as an opportunity to assess the health of your mind. It is important to remember that our thoughts are not always factual. Sometimes our thoughts can be opinions about who we are, based on fears that we are carrying. Therefore, the thought diary is an opportunity to address these opinions and evaluate them based on their merit. It will allow you to dispute, examine, question, and challenge negative thoughts, which oppress your mind and cause distress. Assessing your negative thoughts in your head can be confusing and chaotic; thus, writing them down in an organized manner can help you identify patterns of negative thinking and give you the opportunity to address them.

For this exercise, you will need a blank piece of paper. The first step to addressing your negative self-evaluations would be to briefly write down what you are currently experiencing. For instance, you can identify what situation you are in, what words or phrases you are saying to yourself, and the ways in which you are criticizing or putting yourself down. The second step would be to rate how strongly you believe in these negative thoughts, and how the negative thoughts are making you feel. You can spend time detailing the intensity of your emotions and perhaps previous events in your life where you have felt similar emotions.

After you have completed the first two steps, you will need to challenge your negative self-evaluations. The purpose of challenging your negative self-evaluations is to develop a more balanced outlook. Some of the questions that you can pose to yourself include: what is the evidence for my evaluations? What is the evidence against my evaluations? Are the opinions I have of myself based on facts or opinions? What other perspectives could there be to this situation? What advice would I give to a friend who was in the same situation? Are there any positive factors about me or the situation that I am not seeing? Once you have answered these questions, you can complete the final step, which is to give your negative self-evaluation a new rating. You will rate how much you now believe in this negative self-evaluation, as well as how intensely you feel the emotions that first appeared in the beginning of the exercise.

Chapter Five:

Female Strengths and Gender

Advantages to Make More Use Of

"When I dare to be powerful, to use my strength in the service of my vision, then it becomes less and less important whether I am afraid."

– Audre Lord

Women are powerful when they refuse to doubt their own capabilities. When I count all of the small tasks that only I can perform around the house or in a social context, I am reminded of my own unique strength. Being a woman is not synonymous with being weak, instead, I find that it is synonymous with being powerful, courageous, victorious, and nurturing. While our power may not be as overt as masculine power, I believe that it is more influential and potent. Indeed, we do not need to raise our voice to be heard, yet we can convey a message in the most sincere way, piercing through the most stubborn of hearts. We may not arrogantly boast about our accolades and accomplishments at work, but if you ask us nicely, we will open a file cabinet filled with all of our achievements filed by date in an organized system.

When we are seeking to become more confident and assertive in who we are, we do ourselves a disservice by comparing our strength to that of a man. Our power can only be understood by learning more about the ways that we are different than men. This means that even in the workplace, our strategies of growth will look different. While a man can plan to be more talkative about his role at work and how successful his projects are going, a woman would need to find powerful strategies that would naturally highlight her own progress at work. Below are some of the attributes that make us distinctly feminine, which we can leverage to make us more powerful in both public and private spaces.

10 Things You May Not Have Realized That Women are Better at Than Men

Number one: Women are smarter than men. According to IQ tests conducted around the world, women score higher in Intelligence Quotient than men.

Number two: Women are more sensual than men. According to research conducted by Israel Abramov from the City University of New York, women can see slight variance in color, they have a superior sense of hearing, and can easily decipher between various scents (Jensen, 2015).

Number three: Women have a stronger immune system than men. According to a study done at McGill University, the levels of estrogen in a female body gives women a stronger natural defense against bacteria and viruses (Jensen, 2015).

Number four: Women learn faster than men. A study done at the University of Georgia and Columbia University proved that women were better learners than men and were generally more organized, attentive, and flexible with work (Jensen, 2015).

Number five: Women handle interviews better than men. According to a study carried out in Canada, women were seen to be better at handling the stress of an interview than men were, and only showed signs of nervousness prior to the interview beginning (Jensen, 2015).

Number six: Women graduate from colleges more often than men do. Many studies have shown that female enrollment in college is at a higher rate than male enrollment; however, new research is showing us that women are more likely to successfully complete their degrees and graduate from college than men are.

Number seven: Women are better at managing a workforce of people than men. Women are seen to make better managers because of their natural skill of listening, being empathetic to the needs of others, and multitasking. It has been found that women are socially adept and can readily encourage and direct employees toward a common goal.

Number eight: Women are better at organizing the household finances than men. While most men are believed to be the head of the household, women are by far better administrators of household budgets and tend to be more responsible in saving money for future use. Women are also more aware of how money is used around the house and can therefore find ways of being resourceful in how money is spent.

Number nine: Women are better at following instructions than men. When you give a woman a map or directions on how to assemble a DIY project, she is more likely to understand the instructions and follow the directions without any stress induced. Men on the other hand, are less prone to following instructions, preferring to figure it out on their own—which as a result, makes the process of following directions stressful.

Number ten: Women are better at sustaining relationships than men. Women have been found to put more thought and effort into understanding others, which enables them to have more fulfilling and stronger relationships. A woman will put herself in the other's shoes and attempt to understand their experience of the issue. This quality, along with being amazing mediators, makes a woman a great friend or romantic partner to have.

Hardwired Cognitive Abilities and Behaviors That Science Shows Women Are Better At

Neuroscientists discovered many years ago that the brains of women and men are not identical. Men tend to have a brain that is lateralized, meaning that the two hemispheres of the brain work more independently when men perform certain mental tasks such as communicating or navigating around their present environment. However, in performing the same kinds of tasks, the woman's brain tends to use both of its cerebral hemispheres more equally.

There have also been studies showing the difference in how the brain develops in young girls and boys. For instance, electrical measurements have shown that when infants have reached the three-month mark, boys and girls will respond differently to the sound of humans speaking. Girls were seen to measure higher than boys in both sensory and cognitive development, with hearing, touching, smelling, memory, and vision being more agile in young girls. Girl children are also more socially attuned, allowing them to respond better to human faces, voices, or crying than young boy children.

From the moment that we are born, girls are high-performers and learn how to navigate this world a lot sooner and with more grit than young boys. Knowing how naturally proficient we are from an early age allows us to find the confidence within ourselves to reveal more of our unique qualities. There are many areas that we excel in compared to men, which gives us an upper hand to navigate our way to the top of the corporate ladder, become influential in our communities, or simply in maximizing the value that we share with others. Below are some areas in which we can scientifically claim superiority over men.

Memory

Psychologists and researchers have found that women have a better memory than men. In particular, women were seen to have a better episodic memory, which helps them remember people, time, locations, objects, and conversations that they have heard or have been a part of more clearly. One significant study was conducted at Karolinska Institute and analyzed 617 studies from 1973 to 2003 consisting of over 1.2 million participants overall (Nugumanov, 2019). This major study found that women have better cognitive skills in remembering verbal information such as recalling words, texts, movies, and discussions. By having a good memory, women can easily learn new skills, enroll in an online course, experience improved social interactions, and gain higher confidence in problem solving.

Emotional Intelligence

Women score higher in emotional intelligence than men. In a study carried out by Korn Ferry and Hay House, data was collected from 55,000 corporate professionals across the country and across all levels of management between the period of 2011 to 2015 (Le, 2018). Female managers scored higher in self-awareness, empathy, and having a positive outlook on work. Women also scored higher in mentorship, coaching, teamwork, and adaptability. Emotional intelligence is a strength that many women can take advantage of in their professional lives. It can help women improve on the amount of influence they have at work, the quality of their relationships with co-workers, and in becoming better team leaders or supervisors.

Personality Traits

The innate personality of women can also play to their advantage. Women are known to be naturally agreeable, warm, nurturing, compassionate, and open with their feelings. These natural qualities can be an asset in people-focused businesses, charitable work, social work, and any other field demanding engagement with people, understanding how others think and processing information, or caring for others.

Willpower and Resilience

Women are seen to be more resilient than men. This resilience is seen from an early age, when girls are expected to perform better than boys.

Resilience is built through coping with small-scale stressors presented in the environment that young girls are able to learn from. As the young girl becomes a woman, she is presented with even more stressors, which come from being excluded from accessing privileges that are reserved for men. Other stressors that women are expected to handle include the pressure of having children, getting married, or finding a decent paying job. Nonetheless, resilience is also a gift because it encourages women to persevere through difficulty and build mental toughness. Women can use their resilience to create meaningful goals, and make decisive decisions on how to attain them. Alternatively, women can use their resilience to gain a new skill, cope with stress from work, or decide to further their education.

Intuition

Women are biologically more intuitive than men due to having a larger and more active insula. The insula is a part of the brain that is involved with emotional awareness and empathy. The reason why the insula is more active in the female brain than male brain is due to the high prevalence of the hormone estrogen in women. Being naturally more intuitive allows women the advantage of reading people's facial expressions and emotional undertones of their speech better. This can prove beneficial in work environments as well as in a woman's home life, where communication skills are vital. It can also help women intuitively know which decisions will be profitable or which relationships are built on authenticity and which are not.

Communication

Women are hands down better communicators than men. Due to our high emotional intelligence, we are able to communicate ideas and express information in a more dynamic and inspiring way. Women are able to see many sides of a situation and thus we can present comprehensive information, strategies, and plans, which have considered both the advantages and disadvantages of a situation. From an early age, young girls are able to articulate themselves better than young boys and furthermore, young girls were found to be early adopters of writing. Being an effective communicator can help women express who they are with more confidence and gain favor in the job, club, team, or community circle that they are in. Effective communicators are also more likely to be considered for promotions and raises because their influence is articulated in all of their tasks and in their performance.

Survivors

If none of the points above help you to see your true worth, you can rest assured that this last one will. All women, regardless of social background, educational level, cultural heritage, or religious associations are survivors. We were built to survive adverse circumstances and overcome them with grace. Biologically, our naturally strong immune system helps us to ward off illnesses and live longer and healthier lives than men. This means that despite the oppression that we may face in our environments, we were built to endure and successfully overcome. I have heard many stories throughout my life of women who went from rags to riches, or from slums to using a gavel in a courtroom, and all of this because their temporary circumstances could not restrain them forever.

Reader Task: Lean Into Your Strengths

In this chapter, I have exposed you to some of the many ways in which you are powerful as a woman. Understanding your unique strengths and abilities will encourage you to find new and empowering ways of sharing your skills, knowledge, and talents with others. I find that the more a person shares what is unique to them with others, they are able to gain more confidence in their own abilities. Therefore, I encourage you to quit hiding that amazing singing voice, or your impressive analytical skills. As inferior or overrated as you might think these qualities are, I can guarantee you that there is at least one person within your community who could benefit from some of the strengths that come so naturally to you.

Therefore, for this exercise, I would like you to take a clean sheet of paper and write down the qualities and strengths that make you valuable. Perhaps you believe you are valuable because you can give great advice, work well under pressure, intuitively understand children, or perhaps you can speak many languages. The next step will require you to examine how this list of values can positively impact three levels of your life namely; your own personal development and growth, the relationships you have with others, and the investment you can make in your community or at work. For instance, you may propose that working well under pressure can benefit you personally because it can relieve you of stress. On a relationship level, it can allow you to handle different personalities with ease and display resilience in conflict situations. On a community or work level, your ability to work well under pressure can inspire you to seek more challenges at work, or finally request a promotion because you are able to handle more responsibilities.

Chapter Six:

Fake It 'Til You Make

It/EFT/Visualization

"I always did something I was a little not ready to do. I think that's how you grow. When there's that moment of 'wow, I'm not really sure I can do this,' and you push through those moments, that's when you have a breakthrough."

— Marissa Mayer

It took a lot of going back and forth to decide on finally pursuing my writing career. On the one hand, I didn't have a job to return to, and the thought of applying for another corporate position was stressful. I believe in my mind I had already ruled the old way of working and doing things out. However, what was I going to spend my time doing now? I had a sea of opportunities in front of me—and the more I grew in self-confidence, the greater the amount of opportunities I saw. Writing was always top 5 on the list of dream jobs that I could pursue, but for some reason, the thought of becoming an author made me hesitant.

I remember reading a magazine article on one particular occasion which spoke about building confidence through faking it. At first, I didn't take it seriously, I mean, who would want to pretend to be comfortable in who they are? It sounded quite desperate and counterproductive until I read further. The article wasn't proposing that I become the superficial version of me; instead it presented a solution for self-improvement. The solution was to fake being confident about your tasks or who you are, until you become that version of yourself. By faking, it proposed that you channel the confidence inside of you and not from within your environment. Eventually, you would learn how to become confident naturally and thus, you wouldn't need to pretend to be.

I decided to give it a go and used this advice to encourage me to pursue my writing. I started faking the confidence of a writer; I wrote articles, blog posts, reviews, and shared my opinion as if somebody asked for it. I started exploring the particular topics I loved to write about and I made sure that I had an article on it. I would read my articles aloud to friends and family and they would always spark a meaningful discussion. After a few months of faking it, I had forgotten about my shy and hesitant self who could not bring herself to even admit she loved to write. Faking confidence was not as phony as I had thought; instead, I found that it helped me focus on practicing my craft without the fear of being inadequate or unqualified over my shoulder. By seeing myself as an author, I was willing to challenge myself and take on more opportunities—I was able to leap out of my comfort zone and not feel awkward for doing so.

Part of achieving success involves conveying confidence. Without displaying a ray of confidence, it would be challenging to be acknowledged at work, land a date with your dream man, or make a good impression in front of new people. Even though it pays to be a good person, it is also valuable to seem good or display your goodness to others. Everyone in our society—from businesses to individuals—is on the lookout for value. The reason why we are so attracted to value is that it makes us feel good about ourselves. Therefore, being talented and smart will serve you well when you decide to display your talents and smarts. Even when you are on your journey to building confidence, coming across as a person of value will help you succeed in your relationships with others.

The old adage of "faking it until you make it" is a kind of motivation for those individuals who are not naturally confident. The good news is that they too can take advantage of the opportunities that are accessible for confident people, by seeming confident as well. It takes a lot of practice and personal growth to become a confident person, however, that does not necessarily mean that the doors of opportunity should be closed to you. You can simply visualize the kind of confidence it would take for you to start a project or introduce yourself to a new person, and imagine yourself to have that confidence already in you. Once you have successfully taken the first step with borrowed confidence, you will be empowered to take another step forward with even more borrowed confidence. Soon enough, you won't have to borrow any more confidence because it will all be a part of your newly defined character.

Body Language for Confidence

Amy Cuddy, who is a social psychologist, released an empowering TED Talk discussing how non-verbal communication (or body language) in how others perceive our level of confidence and our own capabilities (Solomon, 2016). Her talk was based on a research study she and her team conducted, where they studied how people performed in job interviews when they did and didn't strike a power pose in the beginning of the interview. The study found that participants that performed the power pose in the beginning of the interview received higher ratings in passion, enthusiasm, confidence, and authenticity in comparison to the group that did not perform the power pose. I am sure you are wondering what this power pose looks like. Well it is quite simple: you put your hands on your hips, feet firmly planted on the floor, and arms flung out making a V-like shape. Cuddy's research proves to us that we can change the perception that people have of us by simply being aware of our body language.

Body language can also help us understand non-verbal communication shared by others. One of my ex-coworkers, Lucy, came back to her desk very discouraged after a follow-up meeting with her manager. When I asked her what was wrong, she said that her manager would not sign off on her product proposal because of some discrepancies with it. She seemed very confused by her boss's decision because according to her, she had been in a previous meeting with him and he seemed positive about the work that she was doing. She took his non-verbal cues of looking at his watch frequently and staring out of the window a few times as a way to show her that he was very busy and thus, the meeting had to be short. Nonetheless, she chose to hold onto his words when he said "I am sure this project will get the go ahead."

I believe if Lucy had taken her manager's non-verbal cues seriously, she would have known that he was not entirely convinced about her product proposal in the first place. In this case, the non-spoken communication was more valuable than what he eventually communicated with his words. Understanding body language will allow us to read the hidden messages that others communicate all of the time. Body language is simply an unspoken language that we are always using to communicate our deeper thoughts and emotions. Some of the ways that we pick up on these unspoken messages is through facial expressions, gestures, body positions, and posture. Being able to effectively read body language can be advantageous for us because it will enhance our awareness of what others are communicating to us. This in effect, will strengthen the reactions and messages we choose to send back to them.

I also find that people who are able to read body language become intuitive about how others will respond, and therefore can easily project a desired emotion or response such as positivity, passion, or friendliness. For instance, if you were approaching an individual with their arms crossed, you would intuitively read their demeanor as being anxious or resistant. Knowing this information would allow you to present yourself as non-threatening, engaging, and warm, in order to allow the individual to feel comfortable speaking to you. Picking up on negative non-verbal signals is a superpower in a work environment, where tension and conflict is prevalent. Difficult conversations, nasty customers, sexist managers, or aggressive coworkers can be a challenge to deal with in a healthy manner, especially when their behaviors catch you off guard.

Learning how to read negative body language will reduce the nervousness, stress, or tension that you sometimes feel when you approach difficult people. Furthermore, when you understand the reason why coworkers or managers are acting the way that they are (their unspoken message), you will be less offended at their negative behavior. For instance, if you were to have a conversation with a person who has minimal facial movement, or does not make sustained eye contact with you, it would communicate their level of disinterest or disengagement in the conversation, giving you an opportunity to schedule a better time to have it, change the topic, or choose to end the conversation politely. Either way, you will always leave the exchange empowered because you had the upper hand in any unpleasant conversation.

How to Project Positive Body Language

Not only can the awareness of body language help to strengthen the quality of communication you have with others, it can also strengthen the quality of communication you *share* with others. Conveying positive body language will help you communicate your ideas, thoughts, and feelings with greater clarity, thus avoiding sending mixed messages. One of the first opportunities you will have to convey positive body language is during your first encounter with an individual—your first impression. It is true what they say about first impressions; these initial encounters are valuable because they allow people to make their first judgement about who you are. It is challenging to step out of the perception that people first make of you because in their minds, it reflects who you are.

Therefore, your first impressions can be seen as the initial sales pitch that you will make indirectly. In order to make this sales pitch successful, you will need to become more aware of your body language and make the necessary adjustments needed. There are a number of tips that you can hold on to when improving upon your body language. The first tip is that you need to maintain an open posture. All this requires of you is to drop your shoulders, take a deep breath, and relax! When your body is holding tension, it shows in the stiffness or rigidity in your face, shoulders, and chest. Practice sitting upright, keeping your hands resting on your lap when you are sitting down or freely hanging on your sides when you are standing up.

The second tip is to practice giving a firm handshake, however, this can become awkward when it isn't done right. Therefore, practice your firm and intentional grip, making sure that you do not hold on to the other person's hand too tightly or for too long. The third tip is to practice maintaining great eye contact—great eye contact goes well with a firm handshake too. Once again, try to avoid maintaining eye contact for long periods at a time because you may look dazed (which looks as though you are not paying attention). I would recommend maintaining eye contact for a few seconds at a time, which will show the other person that you are engaged with the conversation.

The fourth tip is to avoid touching your face. This tip will certainly be difficult for most people to follow because studies have found that the average person touches their face more than 16 times in an hour. Not only is touching your face unhygienic, it can also make you come across as being a dishonest person or lacking in confidence in the message that you are conveying. While this may not always be the case (sometimes it is out of habit), it is still preferable that you avoid fiddling with your hair, placing your hand on your chin or cheek, or touching your nose or forehead.

Acting "As If" Technique

Fear is perhaps one of the easiest emotions to detect in another person. You can detect a person's fear through their inability to maintain eye contact, their inability to stand still, or through the look of sheer panic and terror in their eyes. In the corporate environment, being seen as trustworthy is a way in which others can have confidence in us to lead or complete certain tasks. When we look fearful, we can come across as untrustworthy, unintelligent, and not a fit for the particular company's work culture. Of course, it would be naive of us to think that no one in top level management ever becomes doubtful of their own capabilities or their own performance at work. I can guarantee you that as much as fear is detestable in the corporate environment, it is present all around you. Indeed, most of your leaders will be fearful at times, however, you will never have the privilege to see it.

This is because they have mastered the practice of acting as though they are not fearful. Acting "as if" is a powerful technique to build confidence and gain trust at work. The name of the technique clearly explains what is expected of you—to act as though you are what you desire to be. The emphasis here is on acting, because those who become successful at using this technique are not as confident as they act. You will be glad to know that you do not need a drama degree to become successful at projecting your desired character; all you need is the commitment to take advantage of your natural mental and emotional responses to posture and behavior, in order to project a feeling of natural confidence.

When you lack confidence in completing a task, your mind automatically perceives the task as being beyond your control, or powerless to successfully manage or overcome. In response to this mental perception that is created, you respond emotionally with self-doubt, anxiety, or feeling inadequate. Your body will then process these emotions and react with negative body language such as slouching, being jittery, or avoiding eye contact. Your inability to clearly articulate and express yourself in these moments of fear will further assert that the situation is beyond your control and thus, the cycle of fear and doubt continues.

The acting "as if" technique seeks to reverse the cycle of fear by changing what you think about the situation and thus adjusting your responses. The first step in mastering this technique is to change your posture and instead of shrinking or slouching, assert yourself by standing or sitting upright. The second step involves changing your pace of breathing. When you are nervous about something, your breathing tends to accelerate and your breaths become short and shallow. Adjusting your breath can inspire confidence because it restores the natural calm and soothing breath, allowing you to feel in control of your body and to think more clearly. To adjust your breathing, inhale air through your nose deeply and slowly exhale breath through your mouth deeply and gradually. As you exhale, relax the muscles in your neck and shoulders and allow your body to feel light.

You can continue the process of acting "as if" by choosing to wear clothing that reflects the image and vision that you hope to achieve. For instance, if you one day desire to become a manager, do not delay in dressing the part, walking tall at work, and addressing coworkers the way a manager would. You can also explore different outfits, makeup, colors, and textures that make you feel confident in your body and bring out your radiant beauty. Clothing can become a secret weapon in sending a powerful message about the goals that you hope to one day accomplish. Find inspiration on a power look that is appropriate for the desires you hope to achieve in magazines, through the relationships that you have built, or by identifying famous women who have built a powerful image in your community or globally.

Lastly, the most valuable step in acting "as if" is to relearn how to speak to yourself. It is of no use for you to invest so much effort in looking the part and adjusting your body language if your internal dialogue is negative. What you say to yourself truly matters in convincing others that you are confident. This is because your perception of yourself is influential in how you present yourself to others. If you believe that your new powerful image is embarrassing and ugly, it will be impossible for you to convince others that it is impressive and impactful. You are your biggest critic, and the quality of thoughts and words that you have about yourself can empower you to show a confident demeanor or make you withdraw and feel unworthy. You need to encourage yourself to embrace this new challenge of acting as if you are brilliant because soon enough, you will grow into a woman who is exactly that.

Overcoming Body Image Issues

Research studies have found that people who are more accepting of their bodies tend to keep weight off and maintain a healthy body. However, body acceptance is a challenge that many women and men will grapple with at some stage in their lives. According to Eating Disorders Victoria, approximately 45% of women and 23% of men who are within a healthy weight range believe that they are overweight, and at least 20% of women who are underweight believe that they are in fact, overweight (Eating Disorders Victoria, 2018).

There is certainly a prevalent fear among women that the size of our bodies disqualifies us from enjoying certain privileges in life. These fears are sadly not made up. Our society places tremendous pressure on women to present themselves in a particular way or face harassment from the vicious media or gawking onlookers. The standards of beauty are constantly changing and nowadays, even women who have a thinner frame find themselves ashamed of not having luscious hips or bigger breasts. You would drive yourself insane if you attempted to keep up with societal standards and trends of beauty and therefore it is better to not even try.

Overcoming body image issues requires us to stop trying. Stop trying to fit into those skinny jeans that every other woman is wearing, stop trying to contour your cheekbones to make your face look thinner, stop trying to make your breasts bigger by wearing insertable bra cutlets. Just stop for a minute and consider yourself as being enough. You are enough as you are with frizzy or kinky hair, discolored skin, thighs that touch, teeth that don't touch, and all of the other "imperfections" that you can list. We praise being unique when we speak about presenting ourselves to the world, yet being unique in our appearance is almost shameful. We must challenge this belief and choose to set ourselves free from the policing of our bodies at the hands of society. Instead of following trends that encourage us to hide or mask certain aspects of who we are, we must choose to rather follow those trends which encourage us to *celebrate* who we are.

A negative body image can lead to experiences of depression, shyness, or being self-conscious within intimate relationships. It can also make you lose confidence in your ability to express who you are with others. For instance, a quarter of a woman's self-esteem was found to be linked to her perceptions of her body. Negative perceptions about the body when left unchallenged can further lead to mental illnesses such as body dysmorphia and eating disorders. It is time that women befriend their bodies and learn to love what makes their bodies so special. Our bodies are true masterpieces; the intelligence and beauty of the female body is epitomized in how it is designed to bring life into the world. Our scars are a mark that we have lived and have overcome the most treacherous of circumstances. Our birthmarks make us look distinct from other people and give us wonderful stories to share.

There are four tips that you can begin to practice that will help you overcome your negative body image. The first tip is to quit avoiding your body. The truth is that your body will continue to be your home for the rest of your life, so quit avoiding that it is there. Get to know every lump and bump that you have and start to embrace it as a part of you. If you are somebody who avoids looking at themselves in the mirror, try to step out of your comfort zone by making it a daily practice to look at your entire frame in the mirror and find new body parts to marvel at. You can also practice feeling comfortable touching your body. A great way to practice this is through purchasing body butter and gently massage it onto your skin, paying attention to each part of your body.

The second tip is to stop checking for imperfections on your body because everyone has them and they are not going anywhere. Checking for imperfections is disempowering because it activates a negative internal dialogue, making us feel defeated or unworthy of love and affection. Some of the checking behavior that we can also commit to letting go of is pinching our fat, trying to remove scars or pimples, sucking in our stomachs when looking at ourselves in the mirror, or touching our hair to find split ends. The third tip is to stop comparing yourself to other women. Comparison breeds a similar negative and disempowering feeling as checking yourself.

The unfortunate truth is that this behavior has been reinforced by our society through the media and the rise of influencers and celebrity culture. It can cause harmful body image issues and make us feel inferior to other women, or as though we need to look like our role model before we can claim our own power. One of the ways in which we can combat comparison is to become aware of the times when we are triggered to compare ourselves to another woman, the cause of our trigger, and the internal dialogue that we have with ourselves when we do it. Challenge this negative internal dialogue and ask whether it is a fair assessment and how it makes you feel about yourself.

The fourth tip is to check the assumptions that you have about your body. There is a tendency for women to interpret natural and common phenomena as fatness. For instance, thighs that touch, a stomach that wobbles, stretch marks on areas where you have gained and lost weight, and uneven skin tone are all natural occurrences that happen to all women. Our bodies were built to last us a lifetime and that means that sometimes, we will have wobbling skin or stretch marks that visit and end up staying. Another natural occurrence is bloating, especially during the premenstrual period when our bodies retain a lot of fluid. It is important for you to notice when the assumptions that you have about yourself are imagined and unrealistic, and to do your own Google fact check or consult with your doctor in order to confirm that what you are experiencing is normal and natural.

Tap Into EFT to Change Your Inner Critic

When you close your eyes, which area of your body screams the loudest? For me it is always my mind. As soon as my eyes close, I am bombarded with a wave of thoughts; all of them competing for my attention. I think about my day, what I did, what I still plan to do, the upsetting conversation I had with my husband yesterday, what this upsetting conversation will lead to, what I intend on cooking for dinner, and so forth. Together with the regular thoughts that are focused on the activities and tasks that I need to do, I am also approached by self-destructive thoughts which come with a sinister agenda. These self-destructive thoughts come to criticize my work, progress, relationships that I have with others, my schedule, and other choices that I continue to make.

These thoughts will always review the contributions that I make to my family, work, and community as not being enough, or worthy of acknowledgment. I always find it so surprising how far we allow these negative thoughts to dig deep at our confidence. Sometimes, even though we know that our self-destructive thoughts are a lie, we entertain them and follow the downward spiral that they take us through. It is even more surprising how positive thoughts are never as obsessive and demanding of our attention and time as negative thoughts are. A positive thought comes to the forefront of our mind, gives us a burst of energy and vitality, and swiftly disappears. Negative thoughts on the other hand, love to overstay their welcome and linger in our minds until they have stripped us of our motivation to make any progress forward.

Part of claiming your power and confidence as a woman will involve clearing your mind of the unnecessary self-talk that seeks to weigh you down. When you decide to reduce the mental noise in your head, you will experience a reduction in overthinking which can lead to stress, depression, anxiety, and other mental illnesses. One of the useful tools that you can use to reduce the mental noise in your mind is EFT. EFT stands for Emotional Freedom Technique and it is a method that can be used to eradicate negative self-talk. It involves tapping on acupuncture points along your body, including your face and upper body, while declaring positive affirmations about your life, work, relationships and any other area of your life prone to negativity.

The acupuncture points which you tap during an EFT session represent the points in your body where both physical and psychological energy flows. Typically, when we are experiencing tension in our body or feeling disempowered, it signifies that these energy pathways are blocked and life-producing energy cannot flow to vital parts of our body. Through an exercise known as tapping, we are able to release blocked energy and restore balance and health in our mind, body, and soul. As mentioned above, many people practice EFT along with declarations of positive affirmations. The affirmations address the particular situation that is bringing disharmony in your body and as you tap the body part correlated to your symptoms, the blocked energy is released.

How Does Tapping Work?

EFT tapping works similarly to acupuncture in the sense that it focuses on the meridian points, or the energy hotspots, along your body. However, the two methods differ in how they release blocked energy; acupuncture uses needles to release trapped energy in the affected meridian points, whereas EFT tapping uses the pressure from the fingertips to release trapped energy. Individuals who are proponents of EFT tapping believe that the tapping technique is useful in helping you access your body's energy pathways and send positive signals to the brain to circulate new information throughout the body.

EFT tapping can be broken down into five steps. For every negative belief, emotion, or thought, you will be required to repeat this five-step sequence in order to resolve each issue individually. The first step is to identify the issue at hand. In order for the EFT technique to be effective, you need to identify a clear negative thought or fear that you have and desire to release or reduce the intensity of. This issue will remain your focal point throughout the entire exercise. The second step is to test the initial intensity of this issue. This simply means that you will need to rate the degree of pain that this issue is causing physically or psychologically in your body out of a scale from 0 to 10, with 10 being the most painful or difficult feeling.

Creating a benchmark of the initial intensity will also help you in assessing how much of the pain has been reduced after every EFT sequence. For instance, if your intensity began at 10 and after the sequence was complete, you recorded it at a 5, this would indicate that you have achieved a 50% improvement rate. You can decide after a few weeks to continue improving on this benchmark by completing another sequence on the same issue you had. The third step is to establish a phrase that clearly addresses the issue that you are attempting to heal. Each phrase will be different for each individual, however, all phrases should clearly acknowledge the issue, and show an acceptance of yourself despite having this issue.

For instance, you can create your phrase using this template, "even though I have (your issue or fear), I genuinely and completely accept who I am." Moreover, when creating your phrase, it is important to make sure that the issue is something that you are experiencing and not someone else's issue. For instance, you cannot say "even though my husband cheated on me, I genuinely and completely accept who I am." The correct way to phrase a similar issue would be to say "even though I feel rejected from my husband's cheating, I genuinely and completely accept who I am." It is crucial that you focus on how the problem makes you feel in order to release the conflict and toxicity that it has created in your body.

The fourth step involves performing the tapping sequence. There are 12 meridians that reflect each part of the body and correspond to a particular vital organ. Nonetheless, EFT focuses on 9 of those meridians namely; the karate chop (small intestine meridian), crown of the head (governing vessel), eyebrow (bladder meridian), side of the eye (gallbladder meridian), underneath the eye (stomach meridian), underneath the nose (governing meridian), chin (central vessel), beginning of the collar bone (kidney meridian), and underneath the arm (spleen meridian). As you tap each meridian point, declare a reminder phrase to help you maintain focus on the issue at hand. For instance, if your setup phrase was "even though I feel rejected from my husband's cheating, I genuinely and completely accept who I am," your reminder phrase can be "the rejection I feel that my husband cheated."

You can repeat the sequence for as many times as you desire, ensuring that you evaluate the intensity of your issue after every completed sequence. Compare the level of intensity at the end of the sequence with the one you recorded in the beginning, and repeat the sequence until you have reached 0 or a level that does not cause any discomfort in your mind, body, and soul any longer.

The Power of Visualization

Visualization is a powerful tool that you can use to create images in your mind that reflect the quality of life you seek to live. It is also powerful in building confidence because as you visualize yourself in a more positive light, your mental thought patterns and beliefs change. I remember practicing the visualization technique years ago when I was ready to find my husband and get married. I engaged all of my senses in building a mental image of a man who was kind, considerate, hardworking, and accepted me for who I was. Soon, the mental image of this man was so permanent in my mind, that automatically I began vetting potential suitors with my mental rubric. I didn't waste any time on men who did not fit into the mental image I had of my husband, because it wasn't what I wanted for myself. Eventually, I met Peter and he fit the description to the tee. Every once in a while, I tease him and tell him that I manifested him. The truth is, I probably did and it was all from the power within my own mind.

Visualization is also effective in goal setting. It can help you unlock your imagination and brainstorm ideas and plans for your future. The comforting part about visualizing your goals is that you do not have to be restricted by what you see currently unfolding in your life. Indeed, your visions do not need to be grounded in your current reality; instead it is more empowering to allow your visions to stretch you forward into a more prosperous future. In other words, the quality of your visions will determine your levels of motivation and can-do spirit. Aiming high gives you more drive to accomplish your dream; aiming low keeps you within your comfort zone and thus, doesn't offer you as much inspiration. For the confidence that you seek, I encourage you to visualize a future that is brilliant without any presence of barriers in your success in your personal and professional life.

The first step to successful visualization is to visualize the kind of goal you desire to accomplish. All of us have some kind of inclination of how we desire to live our lives in the most peaceful and meaningful way. Even if we cannot articulate what we want, we do, to an extent, know what makes us happy or what drives our ambition. I also find people who know exactly what they want, however, their current reality distracts them from going ahead with their plans. Typically, they are distracted by sudden crisis, fears, or the pressure from taking on a lot of responsibility in their lives. Once again, visualization does not require us to have a perfect life before we can imagine one for ourselves.

In fact, the purpose of visualization is to guide us toward attaining our so-called "perfect" life. Therefore, whether you can articulate your desires or not, or whether your life seems perfect right now or not, you can begin visualizing a successful tomorrow. I am going to take you through a visualization meditation script that you can practice at home or at work, which will help you activate your imagination and begin attracting goodness in your life. Before I take you through this script, ensure that you are in a quiet and isolated room where you can rest for a few minutes without any interruptions.

Ensure that you are seated in an upright position with your shoulders relaxed and your arms resting on your lap or on your sides. Take a few deep and slow breaths in and out, releasing tension from your entire body. Use your slow and deep breathing to slow your mind until your thoughts gradually quiet down. Once you feel relaxed, I would like you to visualize yourself 5 years from now. See yourself in your future home, the work that you do, and the relationships that you have.

Visualize yourself walking to your computer or laptop and checking your bank balance. See how it is overflowing with money! Notice the emotions that you are feeling at this moment. Notice how proud you are of yourself. In this phase of your life, you do not have any financial issues; all of your needs are met and you do not lack in anything. In this phase of your life, you have achieved greatness; you have overcome tough challenges and now, happiness and confidence are yours to enjoy abundantly. Take a deep and slow breath in and as you exhale, feel the celebration and gratitude for how far you have come in your life. Now, slowly and gently open your eyes and connect with this present moment. You can stay in the same position for as long as you want and reflect on your experience going into the future.

Reader Task: Visualization Continued

Once you have reflected upon your experience visualizing your life 5 years from now, I would like you to take this experience a step further. This exercise will seek to reconcile your past 5 years with the next 5 years of your life. For this exercise, you will need to have a notebook or a journal to document all of your thoughts. Firstly, I would like you to write down all of the milestones that you have accomplished in your past. These milestones will look different for everybody—there are no right or wrong answers here. Once you have a list of your past milestones, for each one, think about the decisions that you had to make in order to achieve them. Perhaps you had to go back to school, adjust your lifestyle, or learn how to budget your money better.

After writing the decisions that were taken to help you achieve these milestones, take it a step further and write down the clarity or realization that you had that allowed you to positively influence your health, relationships, career, or any other area of your life where you achieved notable success. For instance, if your milestone was losing weight, the realization might have been that negative food choices have physical and psychological consequences on your body.

Now turn to the next available clean page in your notebook or journal, and use the confidence of your past successes to set new milestones for the next 5 years. The first step involves writing down the new milestones that you desire to accomplish in the space of 5 years. Do not use your mind too much when creating these milestones, instead refer to the experience you had in your visualization meditation to help you create meaningful milestones. Reflect on how you felt in your future home, and the emotions that erupted inside of you when you checked on your bank balance. With this experience in mind, create milestones that you believe will guide you toward your prosperous future.

Once you have successfully created your future milestones, for each one, write down the decisions that you need to make in order to realize these goals. These decisions will become your blueprint in achieving the milestones that you have created, therefore, it is important to make these decisions as practical, easy to follow, and motivating as possible. Add as much detail as you need in these decisions so that you have a comprehensive blueprint to follow. After writing down the decisions that you need to make and follow for each milestone, write down the clarity or realization that you need for each in order to power you with the confidence to achieve it. For this step, you can search for wisdom, facts, or truths about yourself or the milestones that you want to achieve that will empower you to accomplish your goals. You can also document case studies of women you have seen succeed in the same milestones that you are hoping to achieve, which will encourage you to remain committed and resilient on your journey.

Part Three:

The Right Time and Place for

Employing Assertiveness Skills

Chapter Seven:

Assertiveness at Work

"Justice is about making sure that being polite is not the same thing as being quiet. In fact, oftentimes, the most righteous thing you can do is shake the table."

— Alexandria Ocasio-Cortez

Many people misunderstand what it means to be assertive at work. Many times, assertiveness in the work environment is confused with being aggressive or dominant with others. As I have mentioned in this book, assertiveness is not synonymous with aggressiveness; the two behaviors couldn't be more different from each other. Aggressive behavior at work is a struggle for power and control over others and situations, whereas assertiveness at work is a declaration of your own power while having an awareness of community. Everybody desires to work in an environment where they are seen and their contribution is acknowledged. Nonetheless, research studies continue to show us that most employees feel powerless and subjugated to unfair practices at work.

One of the reasons why employees feel powerless is due to their lack of confidence in expressing themselves with clarity and conviction to others. This feeling of powerlessness becomes more pronounced as an employee rises in position within the organization without finding solutions earlier in their career. Identifying your communication style and adjusting it accordingly is a great solution for regaining power at work. The most sought-after communication is assertiveness, because it allows people to express themselves in a healthy manner that lets both parties leave the conversation having been heard. If you think about your own work environment, you will see examples of communication gone wrong.

Firstly, you will identify that person whose shyness or uncertainty in their tasks has resulted in them being overlooked or seen as weak. You will also identify that person whose attempts at being assertive has led to aggressive behavior, thus making them overlooked and labelled as not being a team player. These two common profiles of workers are found in most organizations because, let's face it—being assertive is not easy. It is especially not easy for women at work to assert themselves and it isn't necessarily due to our natural disposition as women. Professor Daniel Ames from Columbia Business School found that the range of latitude for women at work is much smaller in what they can get away with (Experteer Magazine, 2018). This means that part of the reason why women find it difficult to assert themselves is due to the fear of being punished for their boldness for the same things that men would be rewarded or celebrated for.

For instance, when a woman is a team leader, she will have to face perceptions of either being too pushy or, on the other extreme, being a pushover. Furthermore, women find it difficult to assert themselves at work due to their traditional roles of being peacemakers, which leads to passive behaviors and as a result, missed opportunities for growth or leadership within the organization. Therefore, as much as there are many factors within the work environment that seek to silence the power of women, we need to fight to be heard and express ourselves in the most authentic ways.

When to Be Assertive With Your Team

It is important for women to learn how to be assertive in teams because usually, that is where talent is identified and sourced. Being able to express your needs and wants in a team environment will boost your confidence and allow you to express your voice and unique attributes for everybody to see. Drawing out your assertiveness will depend on how well you understand your personality. In other words, the greater the amount of self-awareness you have, the greater the amount of insight you will have in dealing with other personality types. Within a team, you will always find those members who express themselves differently to you, however, this should not be seen as a mountain. Rather, it should be seen as an opportunity to use your assertiveness skills in bridging what seems to be a gap in communication.

Being assertive will move you away from the role as victim to the role as victor, as you navigate difficult situations and difficult people with confidence and unwavering strength. Assertiveness within your team will make others identify you as a natural leader as you become the go-to person for encouragement, mediation, and vision. It will teach you the power of effective collaboration, having the ability to bring out the talents of each team member and using them to improve upon the projects at hand. Assertive communication will effectively remove the "I" in group work and allow team members to see themselves as a collective, being stronger when working and sharing ideas together.

There are many tips that you can start implementing in finding your voice within teams at work, thus becoming more assertive. The first tip is to learn how to read patterns. This requires understanding situations where you feel restricted from sharing your thoughts and feelings, situations where you feel powerless, as well as situations where you feel you have to be aggressive. Recognizing the common patterns of how you communicate with others and in what contexts will help you plan a tactful and assertive response going forward. The second tip is to align your verbal and non-verbal communication in order to strengthen your message.

For instance, check to see if your body language is reiterating your spoken language through strong eye contact, posture, and confident gestures. It would also be useful to plan what you would like to say before you speak, in order for your words to come out clear and offer a valuable and well-considered message. For instance, in a meeting you can choose to write down all of the points you wish to raise, and plan how and when you would like to raise these points within the meeting.

When the time comes, you will be able to speak confidently, having a clear guideline of what you desire to say.

The third tip is learning how to pick your battles appropriately. I can guarantee you that there will be conflict among team members because of there being so many different personalities. It is important for you to understand which disagreements are worth debating over and which ones are worth disengaging in. Being involved in constant fighting will lead to aggressive behavior and thus, make you lose the respect and trust that you have built with your team members. Furthermore, involving yourself in every dispute within the team will lead to you developing a reputation for being disruptive to the progress of the team.

Therefore, only focus on conflicting points that will affect the progress or performance of the team, and choose to ignore conflicting points that are not related to the work at hand. If the conflict involves all team members, choose to discuss the issue democratically, allowing for all voices to be heard. Alternatively, if the conflict involves one member of the team, request a meeting in an informal environment where both of you can share your viewpoints and negotiate the best way forward.

The LADDER Model

Imagine that you are at work, preparing for an important company meeting involving all employees from every department and level of seniority. You are excited to be a part of this meeting because you have been told that there is exciting news that your director will share with all staff members. As you make your way to the meeting room, you are called by your manager who firmly says "we cannot have the phones left unattended, would you please stay behind and monitor the incoming calls?" The truth is that you are offended by this request because you have every right to be a part of this inclusive company meeting, however, you politely smile and tell your manager that you will gladly assist. As all of your coworkers leave for the meeting, you are left with bitter regret, asking yourself why you have allowed blatant disrespect from your manager once again.

Some of you may have experienced a similar scenario in your own work environment, which left you feeling disempowered and undermined by your colleagues. The good news is that through this book, you have learned how to identify your passive behaviors and ways of becoming more assertive. The most empowering aspect about gaining assertiveness is that it allows you to say "no" and feel confident doing so. You are able to express your thoughts without feeling as though you are bothersome or inconveniencing others. Instead of believing in self-sacrifice and an unhealthy degree of compliance, you are encouraged to believe in win-win situations where work relationships are built on respect, humility, and an acceptance for others.

In situations where you are tasked to resolve an issue assertively, you can make use of the LADDER model. The LADDER model is a straightforward mnemonic framework that you can use when you desire to express your opinions and thoughts with others in a more confident manner. There are six steps involved in the model which you can follow sequentially. The "L" represents looking at your rights in the situation. This is an important first step because when you understand your rights—such as the right to be heard, the right to express yourself, or the right to be respected—you are able to see where the problem lies and how to go about requesting what you need.

The "A" represents arranging a meeting. Arranging a meeting is important because sometimes it is inappropriate to have an assertive conversation in that moment. Moreover, arranging a meeting formalizes your dispute and allows for the other person or people involved to respect your time. The "D" represents defining the problem at hand. Before your arranged meeting, it is necessary to plan what you would like to express to those involved and how you desire to express it. On a piece of paper, clearly detail what the problem is and the ways in which it impacts on your performance at work. Avoid using emotive language when describing the problem in order for the message to be clear and the other person or people to understand your position.

The second "D" represents describing how the problem makes you feel. Once you have laid down the facts in a direct manner, you can proceed to describe how the problem makes you feel. Sharing the emotional impact that the problem presents in your work life allows the other person to appreciate the depth of the problem. For instance, if your problem is with a coworker's sexist remarks, you can share how these remarks reinforce your powerlessness in an already patriarchal society. When you do share your feelings, ensure that you use "I" statements and avoid blaming the other person for your own feelings. For instance, you would say "I feel powerless" instead of "you make me feel powerless."

The "E" represents expressing what you desire to see happen going forward. Prepare a short summary of the expectations or outcomes that you desire to see happen. These outcomes should be presented as a solution, however, express your willingness to compromise or negotiate a joint solution, which would include the suggestions made by the other person or people. The "R" represents reinforcing the mutual benefits of the solution that has been suggested. Express how the agreed upon solution will bring value into the work relationship that you have with the other person or people, and frame the solution as being an overall win-win for both parties.

Assertiveness in Interviews

Discussing interviews is a sore subject because we all have painful memories of interviews gone terribly wrong. Perhaps the most appropriate setting to have displayed assertiveness was in my countless interviews, where confidence played a significant role in making a positive impression. I am certain that if you had a greater amount of confidence and assertiveness, you would willingly apply for more interviews, even for job positions that are outside of your comfort zone. The general rule of thumb when it comes to having a successful interview is to capture the attention of the employer by highlighting yourself as the best candidate for the job.

Fulfilling this mission takes effective communication of your strengths and the qualities that can allow you to succeed in your potential position. In other words, you would need to sell yourself and your skills in the best way possible in order to make a lasting impression. The worst-case scenario in any interview is to display signs of a lack of assertiveness. The ways in which you can do this is by sounding unsure of your abilities, creating an impression of being a people pleaser, or mumbling your words or not offering in-depth responses to questions. Nevertheless, assertiveness is not only required during the interview, it is also important to display before and after the interview has taken place.

Assertiveness should be shown during the first point of contact that you make with your potential employer. For instance, assertiveness would be shown through your application process in how you seek and apply for the position. A confident woman will only seek to work for organizations where she feels she can add value. Choosing an organization based on desperation will blind you to so many factors that can impact your happiness at work. From the onset, you should prioritize your satisfaction rate with the role, the salary that is offered, the work culture of the organization, as well as any benefits or incentives that are offered for that role.

Once you have assessed whether the available post meets your standards for the type of work environment you are looking for, you will need to prepare for the interview. Preparation prior to the interview is key in order to plan what you are going to say and how you are going to say it, in a way that projects confidence and assertiveness. Research potential interview questions and formulate interview answers that would display your confidence in your own abilities and skills. It would also be useful to prepare documents and notes that you intend on taking with you to the interview, such as your resume, references, or evidence of your qualifications.

When you arrive at the interview venue, ensure that you are dressed well, and presented similarly to how someone in the role that you are seeking would present themselves. Before the interview begins, take a few deep breaths and visualize a positive outcome. Visualize yourself answering the questions confidently and impressing the interviewer with every response given. This would also be the best time to release any tension that you have in your body and relax your muscles. When you meet the interviewer for the first time, stand up and warmly greet them, ensuring that your handshake is firm and your demeanor is warm and embracive. You can exchange pleasantries and make small talk until both of you are comfortable in the interview room.

Most candidates will experience difficulty answering behavioral questions asked by the interviewer. These types of questions seek to understand how the candidate reasons and solves problems effectively—in essence, these questions are trying to see how assertive the candidate is in a work and team environment. Answer these questions by sharing previous work stories that highlight moments where you displayed decisive action, problem-solving, collaboration, and conflict resolution. Keep these stories related to the current company and job position that you are seeking, as well as the expectations of this particular role. If you achieved a promotion at your previous job or achieved something impressive, you can mention it and explain how this accomplishment played a role in your performance.

Reader Task: Practicing Role Play Interview Questions

Most interviewers enjoy role playing as part of testing the candidate's fit for the job. Role playing involves the interviewer creating scenarios which the candidates need to find a solution for. The purpose for the role play is to see how the candidate would handle difficult tasks or lead a team in their desired role. Candidates can excel at answering these hypothetical scenarios by offering assertive solutions.

These assertive solutions would emphasize your competence, communication skills, as well as leadership abilities. In this exercise, you will have the opportunity to start practicing how you would approach role play interview questions. Remember that you may not be given these scenarios however, the ones you do receive will always include some kind of controversy at work, conflict, customer complaint, or any other difficult experience typical to the job you are applying for.

Scenario One

You are part of the customer service team of a popular retail group. A customer who had purchased lettuce from one of your stores discovered a slug in the lettuce and is now threatening to take the incident to the papers and report the company to the consumer watchdog. Contact the customer and resolve this dispute.

Scenario Two

You have recently been promoted as executive manager over another manager who is threatening to leave the company and work for your competitors. As executive manager, it is your responsibility to retain as many high-performing managers as you can in the organization therefore, persuade the manager to stay.

Scenario Three

You are the team leader in a group with passive communicators and aggressive communicators. Explain how you would motivate the passive communicators to take a more active role in the team, and how you would convince the aggressive communicators to agree in sharing the platform with others.

Scenario Four

Your manager has placed you on night shift for the third consecutive week without any explanation. This has inconvenienced your personal routines at home because you arrive too late to cook or spend time with your family. Explain the dilemma to your manager and propose a solution that satisfies both of your interests.

Scenario Five

Your manager has introduced a new system of completing tasks which you do not agree with. The new system is complicated, takes up more of your time, and it requires that you change your workflow process. Explain your disapproval of the new system to your manager in an assertive way and propose a better solution.

Chapter Eight:

Assertiveness Outside the Work

Environment

"I raise up my voice—not so that I can shout, but so that those
without a voice can be heard. ... We cannot all succeed when half of us
are held back."

— Malala Yousafzai

You were born to be assertive. From the time when you were a baby,
your natural instinct and way of relating to this world was through
open and honest expression. This is why you were so lovable and
received plenty of honesty and openness in return. However, this
natural assertiveness didn't last long. The moment your thinking brain
began to mature, those around you started creating fear narratives,
which would groom you to fear what they feared and shrink in areas
where they had shrunk. At this point, your caregivers started teaching
you the strategies that they sincerely believed would keep you safe and
protected in life. Nonetheless, by teaching you strategies through their
own lenses of fear, they unwittingly taught you how to behave in non-
assertive ways.

There are four programs that you may have been taught as a child,
which have led to a lack of assertiveness in your adult life. The first is
the blame program. The blame program is a defensive game that you
play when you see the world as hostile and threatening to the love
around you. Other times, the hostility is experienced within you and

thus, you believe that you are loveless. Those who play the blame game decide to blame others in order to protect their own familiar surroundings, routines, or loved ones. Alternatively, the blame game can also be directed internally, blaming yourself for your perceived failure, inadequacy, poor performance, or for the behavior of others.

The second is the false self program. The false self is the image that you create when you believe that being your true self is not enough. The false self therefore is based on an external standard of what is acceptable and what is not, and usually it is created out of a survival instinct. You learn to hide who you truly are and instead, show a diluted representation of yourself. The ego takes charge of your life and your life becomes a commitment to this false mask. The danger of the false self is that it creates its own beliefs, which end up imprisoning the one who believes in them. These are beliefs like; forgiveness is a sign of weakness, anger is a sign of power, or withdrawing love is a way to control or punish others.

The third is the false life script program. As a result of the decisions that you made in your earlier childhood and adolescent age, you would have created a personality which others believe to represent who you are. This personality serves as your label; a kind of identification that others know you by. What makes this identity influential in your life, is that after much practice, you will believe that it represents you too. Even though it is limited and not entirely representative of all that you are and will be, it shapes how you experience your life. When your personality includes destructive habits or negative attributes, you begin to believe that you are naturally negative or naturally shy. Even though this probably isn't the case, the mere fact that this identity is enforced daily makes you believe that it must be true.

The fourth is the personality type program. Nearing the end of your formative years, you would have developed a distinct personality that reflects what you have been exposed to within your community. The type of personality that you develop will determine how you respond to life circumstances, particularly the prevalence of stress or danger in your environment. Referring to the personality typology known as the Enneagram, your personality will fall under one of these predominant categories, namely; the perfectionist, peacemaker, rebel, self-doubter, winner, or observer.

Therefore, how you are raised and the programming which you are groomed under will determine your level of assertiveness in your adulthood. Moreover, the quality of the environment which you were brought up in will also influence your level of assertiveness. For instance, in homes where children are not affirmed of their unique qualities or given emotional support, the children are more likely to grow up doubting themselves and lacking in self-confidence.

Nonetheless, what you could not control as a child, you can control as a grown woman. Instead of counting what you were not given or lamenting on the dysfunctional environment you grew up in, you can decide to start displaying assertiveness in your current relationships. It is not too late to reclaim your power and to change the narrative in your life. Not only do you deserve respect in the office, you also deserve respect at home and among your friends.

Assertiveness with Friends and Family

When you behave more assertively in your relationships, you will feel less worn out when interacting with friends and family due to the healthy boundaries erected. Attending family functions or coffee with your girlfriends won't feel threatening any longer, now that you have found your voice. Those who were comfortable speaking over you or criticizing you every time you decided to share your opinions won't be left unchecked. You will be able to stand your ground and clearly articulate your needs in order to receive the support, love, and compassion that you desire. Of course, there will be those family members or friends who resist this new you. This should not deter you from committing to express your new found power. Soon, they will learn that you mean business and therefore will not compromise on finally living in your truth.

Responding to Criticism

Responding to criticism from relatives or friends can be a challenge for people who are not assertive. They can either assume the passive role and give a submissive reaction, or assume the aggressive role and give a biting reaction. The first thing to remember about criticism is that it is someone else's opinion of you and therefore it really has no weight in determining your progress or performance in your life. Secondly, instead of allowing the criticism to disorient you and make you shrink, choose to ask more questions about the person's assertion. Ask them how they got to this conclusion and the facts that they have based their criticism on to see how much truth lies in their words. If you find that there is no truth in their criticism, you do not need to spend any more time thinking about it.

Saying "No" to Others

Part of being assertive with your relatives and friends involves learning when to say "no." I used to fear refusing my relative's requests because I felt as though they would ostracize me; however, I learned that saying no sometimes will earn you respect and favor from the very same people—nobody values a pushover who commits or agrees to everything. The best way to say "no" is to state it loud and clear up-front and explain that you won't commit to the individual's request.

Expressing Your Feelings

Non-assertive people are usually afraid to express their feelings, fearing humiliation or corrective behavior when they do. This can lead to them undermining their feelings and viewing them as not being important or valuable. You can break the cycle of submissiveness by practicing hearing your own voice. Practice sharing your opinion about a popular series, movie, or social event in the mirror. As you share this opinion, pretend that you are also listening to someone share theirs in return. Affirm their position and respond with a brief summary of your opinion. This exercise will help you build confidence in sharing your views in a group or social setting.

Own What You Say

Sometimes we can get carried away in a conversation and say things without being mindful of the impact that our words carry. One of the most damaging sentences are those that project responsibility on another person; these are typically "you" sentences. "You" messages make others responsible for our feelings, actions, or outcomes in life; instead of assuming complete responsibility for our own life, we make others carry our hurt, disappointment, or regrets. These types of sentences can destroy relationships and therefore it is important to avoid them at all costs. A healthier way to express your hurt to others is to use "I" phrases such as "I feel disrespected when you speak over me."

Assertiveness in Intimate Relationships

It is common to disagree with your boyfriend or spouse in a relationship and feel as though your thoughts and feelings are not considered when certain decisions involving daily living are made. This is normal, and practicing how to communicate your needs (as well as listening better) should resolve the conflict. However, there are times when the relationship experiences an imbalance of power, where one partner is dominant and the other is submissive. This imbalance becomes notable when the dominant partner makes inconsiderate or selfish requests that the submissive partner cannot refuse. Moreover, the imbalance can be seen when the dominant partner speaks over the submissive partner in discussions or criticizes the submissive's views and beliefs.

The submissive partner only tolerates this behavior because they view confrontation as dramatic or too disruptive to the union. The aggressive partner soon controls the direction of the relationship, as well as the behavior of the submissive partner. These types of relationships do not necessarily need to be abusive in nature, but there is a noticeable dysfunction in communication. However, when the control becomes abusive, seeking help is highly recommended in order to restore the balance of power. When the issue is based on non-assertiveness, you can practice some of the following tips.

Reflective Listening

Becoming more assertive in your intimate relationship will require you to improve your listening and responding skills. It is difficult to hold someone accountable for their negative behavior if you are not listening to them speak attentively. It is important for both you and your partner to practice listening to the verbal and non-verbal communication of the other. At all times, ensure that you are being as open and transparent with your body language and spoken words as possible. When you or your partner have finished making a point, practice summarizing what has been said and allowing the speaker to confirm if the summary was a true reflection of their message.

Think Before You Speak

Learn to think about your message before you share it with your partner. Sometimes, our partner will share a thought or feeling that does not require our input or assertion. In fact, in situations like these, it would be inappropriate for us to add our own opinion to what has already been shared. The goal for healthy communication in a relationship is to authentically share how you feel while remaining respectful of the other person. Therefore, think your assertions through by considering if the information you are planning to share can add value or make your partner feel respected and loved.

Collaborative Support

Change is inevitable in our own lives and this message is true even in our intimate relationships. Change experienced while in a relationship can be uncomfortable and lead to misunderstandings or miscommunication. Couples can support each other through periods of change by practicing collaborative support. In simple terms, collaborative support involves both individuals committing to make the necessary adjustments in their lifestyle, habits, or planning to accommodate the new change. For instance, your decision to become more assertive in your career and personal life would become a collaborative goal that you pursue with your partner, supporting each other through your transition. Your partner would help you remain committed and encourage you in many practical ways to continue reclaiming your power.

Assertiveness in Social Settings

We are social creatures and thus, cannot survive in isolation. We crave relationships and new encounters with people because our natural default is to express who we are and share our lives with others. Therefore, our confidence cannot remain in the office, it must extend to all areas of our lives including social settings. Confidence can be a useful quality to have in social settings because it will allow you to confidently introduce yourself to new people, attend networking events, and to boldly sign up with social clubs or groups and meet like-minded people. The following are a few tips that you can follow when becoming more assertive in social settings.

Presenting Yourself

When out on the town, your presentation matters. Without any words expressed, how you dress, your body language, as well as your attitude will send a message to those who may be noticing you. How many times are you aware of the message that you are sending across in public spaces? Most people ignorantly believe that they don't need to make an effort when going out in public, however, this assumption is false. Whether you are aware of it or not, your presentation in social settings represents your personal brand, which many will hold you accountable for. If you desire to be respected socially, ensure that you are presented in a respectable way and you will not struggle receiving the kind of attention you desire.

Avoid Controversial Topics

It is always recommended to avoid controversial topics in social settings because they can offend those who are among you. By entertaining controversy, you are bound to step on a few toes and lose favor from your peers or dampen your reputation. When a controversial topic does arise, choose to not take a stand, however, if you feel compelled to comment, always present both sides of the argument and make a fair and wise opinion.

Give Positive Feedback

Everyone is an acquaintance when beginning a friendship and over time, this acquaintanceship evolves. One of the surest ways to ensure that an acquaintanceship becomes a friendship, is to regularly exchange positive feedback. The best way to give feedback is to comment on natural occurrences or developments within the setting or discussion, without trying too hard to find something to comment on. For instance, you can give positive feedback on the free information that someone shares with you, and make your comment feel genuine. Assertive people are always seeking to find commonalities between themselves and others, and to highlight the goodness that they see in another person.

Reader Task: An Assertive Response to Criticism

When others are critical of our decisions or opinions, we can see it as a personal attack on who we are and thus, it can make us shrink or become aggressive. Both responses are not conducive to a healthy outcome for all parties involved—either we assume the role of the submissive individual or we become dominant. Sometimes, criticism is not intended to harm us but to help us see a situation through a different perspective. Being open to receive criticism displays confidence because we are secure in who we are enough to listen to someone else share their opinions on us or our lives. Listening to them share their criticism does not necessarily mean that we must agree with it. However, it allows us to see the effects of our actions or behaviors through someone else's eyes.

In this exercise, you will practice how to respond assertively to criticism through various scenarios that I will present to you. The first part of the exercise requires you to practice how it feels to respond passively, passive-aggressively, and aggressively to criticism. The purpose of this first part is showing you how the choice of words, phrases, and tone used in a response can change the intention of a sentence. The scenario for the first part of this exercise is: a friend telling you that your outfit does not suit your body type. Use this scenario to create three sentences (using the three different communication styles) in response to this criticism.

Notice how it felt conveying the message in three different styles. What were the words used in each response that triggered these feelings? Imagine the outcomes that each response would create. For instance, how would your passive response influence the relationship that you have with your friend moving forward? For the second part of this exercise, I would like you to use the same scenario to create three new responses. This second batch of responses will respond to criticism in a different way. In these responses, you will make three different assumptions; assuming that the criticism is true, assuming that the criticism is not true, and assuming that the criticism is partly true.

Practice conveying these three assumptions and notice how each one feels when you communicate it. What difference does assertive communication make in presenting each assumption? How has your language differed from the first part of the exercise? Do you feel more empowered by your responses and if so, why? Lastly, I would like you to reflect back on one recent scenario in your real life where you could have responded in a more assertive way to criticism. Notice the different ways in which you could have presented your message. Imagine how differently the outcome would have turned out if an assertive response to the criticism was given.

Chapter Nine:

Keeping Safe

"Women's speech—and the fact that we are now listening to it—has
enraged men in a way that makes them determined to reestablish the
longstanding hierarchy of power in America. ... And yet this awful truth
will not stop women from speaking, and I do not think that it will turn
a movement into a moment. It has become clear that there is not nearly
enough left to lose."

— Jia Tolentino

There are many narratives that women are told to follow in the greater
machinery of patriarchal fear in our societies. Indeed, patriarchy cannot
survive in the absence of the fear it breeds. It tells us to fear men, fear
power, and fear expressing our voice. Fear is how we as women are
kept under patriarchal control and told that we will be safe if we remain
unseen. One of the most disempowering scripts that we hear from our
youth is to start grooming ourselves early in our adolescent years for
later dependency on a man. Marriage is seen to be a safety blanket that
all women should aim for in life, in order to keep safe. Thus, many
women fear being single for long periods of time because they perceive
a lack of security in their lives.

Our dependence on men has fueled patriarchal power and has led to
some men believing that they have control over the female body. Some
researchers have even tried explaining the urge for men to oppress
women as being biological. For instance, a sociologist by the name of
Stephen Goldbery suggested that the inherent competitive nature of
men makes them more aggressive and power-hungry, thus motivating
them to go for the senior positions at work and leaving women to

assume the role of the subordinate. However, I believe that findings like these give men a get-out-of-jail-free card, allowing them to avoid facing the consequences of misusing power.

Women in this age have the privilege to access knowledge that can open their eyes to the gross misconduct and psychological abuse that they have succumbed to for centuries. Movements such as feminism have played a significant role in studying and shedding light on gender inequality in our global society while empowering women to reclaim their power. The Stop Hunger organization found that women empowerment is one of the ways to eradicate hunger and achieve economic progress in communities around the world. This is because an empowered woman can feed an entire village. When our fears have dissolved, we see the hidden potential that was always within us and change becomes possible in our lives. Perhaps this is why an empowered woman is such a threat to the power-hungry man and patriarchal system that has survived for centuries on our subordination.

The War on Feminism: #MeToo Movement

The #MeToo movement began in the United States as a campaign to encourage women who have experienced sexual violence, especially in the workplace, to have a platform where their stories can be heard. The movement soon grew to symbolize hope after experiences of sexual violence, as well as highlighting the importance of standing up against predatory men and refusing to be silenced by fear. It became a movement of female solidarity and for the first time in centuries, women felt powerful in their numbers. This movement was ridiculed by some men who believed that it was an attack on their manhood. You can imagine how threatening a message of accountability can be to a misogynistic man who has built his identity on the privileges of being a man.

The #MeToo movement was merciless in calling out and shaming the oppressors named in these gross claims of sexual violence. Most of these men were in positions of power and had never been brought to court in such a public and humiliating manner before. No longer could they threaten their victims into silence and subordination because an army of women, banded together from across the world, were willing to take the offensive position. Many men (and surprisingly some women) have challenged feminism as being an agent of division, seeking to create a wedge between the two genders. If creating a wedge means empowering women to reclaim their power, then perhaps a wedge is necessary. Those individuals who believe that feminism is a movement of troublemakers are misinformed about the intention of this movement.

If patriarchy is a system of power and control, feminism becomes a threat to this power and control. No man who has enjoyed his gender privileges will willingly let them go without a fight. Thus, we have seen a war on feminism and the various movements and campaigns started around the world. The critics of the movement seek to accomplish the same goal as the patriarchal system: silence the voices of women. It is even more saddening that women are opposing the feminist movement, sighting feminists as being angry and bitter women. Nowadays, I find that women are silencing the voices of other women and labelling their cries as irrational, dramatic, or attention-seeking. Therefore, the war on feminism is not only led by men—it is also led by women that are in positions of power who assert their dominance on other women.

The Pull Her Down Syndrome

The patriarchal society in which we live has led to women competing among themselves for crumbs of power available in the workplace. Instead of looking at another woman as an equal, most power-hungry women will see their sister as being a rival. The competition between women in the work environment is a fight to be seen as valuable or to receive validation from male coworkers. This competition is fueled by a negative belief that there aren't enough opportunities available to be shared among everyone; thus, the only solution is to compete for the scarce resources within the work environment. This belief makes women assume the role of the aggressor and they are typically dominant and territorial in their roles at work.

This phenomenon is known as the Pull Her Down Syndrome, or mockingly nicknamed PhD, due to the senior positions that most women who show signs of this syndrome assume. The Pull Her Down Syndrome reinforces the oppressive dominance of power structures in the work environment, which create barriers for women in lower positions to climb up the corporate ladder. The sad part is that this oppression is led by women in senior management positions who believe that in order to succeed in their roles, they are forced to side with men also in those powerful positions. Some of the symptoms of this syndrome include not being happy when you hear of another woman's success, withholding information that can empower another woman, condescending behavior to women who are of lower ranking, or sabotaging another woman's ideas, plans, or opportunities.

Women can overcome the Pull Her Down Syndrome by challenging the traditional systems of power. Of course, this is a difficult task to undertake in a night and it will require a commitment to challenge the norms and practices that take place in the workplace. Instead of women competing with each other for relevance or validation, they should collaborate on efforts to grow within the work environment and see the success of another woman as a win for the upliftment of an entire gender. We should start seeing each other as partners and equals who have been afflicted by a common oppressive system. Our unity in a work environment strengthens our collective assertions; in other words, when a woman is supported by other women at work, her grievances receive support and change becomes possible.

It is impossible for a woman to succeed alone in the workplace because men will never understand your needs, motivation, or experience of work as much as a woman can. The #MeToo movement is an excellent example, showing that the road to our full emancipation as women must be travelled in solidarity with other women. Regardless of the status, class, or job position that a woman occupies, she is still valuable to your full emancipation. She has walked in your shoes and has experienced similar suffering, making her the perfect ally and friend.

Protection Tips in Public Spaces

As women, we need to lean on each other for safety. We cannot depend on a man's security to keep us safe, especially when we know how much power and control men derive from feeling superior to women. Our bodies may be smaller but our strength is mighty—never forget that you were built to survive. In these treacherous times, where women are raped and murdered on their way home or by their own husbands and boyfriends, it is important for us to make it a practice to share information regarding safety and protection. There are so many tips that we have all heard at some point in our lives that could save another woman's life. As the final offering in this book, I would like to share with you some of the tips that I have practiced over the years as safety precautions in public spaces. Feel free to share these tips with women in your home, friendships circles, and workplaces.

The first tip is to always text your close friend or partner when you are going to a place and when you are on your way home. You can even go as far as sharing your GPS coordinates by sending your location in order for those closest to you to always know where you are. I find that notifying those around you of your coming and going creates a sense of safety, especially when you are travelling to a location you haven't been before or perhaps going on a date with a stranger. You will feel more comfortable exploring the town knowing that at all times, someone close to you can always find you.

A second tip is to pretend to talk on the phone with somebody when you find yourself feeling unsafe in a public space. When predators see you speaking with someone on the phone, they are less prone to approach you, fearing that you will share details of your location and the attack to the one you are speaking to. You can also choose to automatically dial a close friend or relative, however, remain alert and notice any sudden changes in your environment. In situations like this, it is always advised to find the nearest open and public space to head to.

The third tip when feeling unsafe in a public space is to hold your keys wedged in between your fingers, so that you can use them as a tool for self-defense when the circumstance calls for it. If you fear losing your keys, buy a bottle of pepper spray and keep it within close reach whenever you find yourself in threatening social environments. The fourth tip is to accept offers from friends to walk you home or to your car after a night out. When women are seen walking alone at night, it becomes an opportunity for predators to launch an attack. It is also difficult to identify predators in an isolated parking lot and thus, you may not be aware of their nearing approach. When you do not have a trusted friend to escort you to your car, you can ask a security guard or patrolling officer to walk with you.

The fifth tip is to avoid taking public transport at night. Instead, you can opt to catch a ride with a friend who may live within the same neighborhood as you, or alternatively, request the services of an Uber. There is usually very limited security or CCTV cameras in public stations or bus stops and therefore, it presents a danger for women travellers. The sixth tip is to avoid walking past a group of people at night. Even if the group seems non-threatening, their power in numbers can be threatening to a woman walking alone. Choose to cross the road or walk another route when you come across a group.

The seventh tip is to pretend to know a woman who seems to be in danger. This tip can save drunk women from the aggressive advances of opportunistic men who may seek to take her home with them. Notice the body language of the woman who you perceive to be under threat and approach her when you believe that she is powerless in the situation. When you approach her, pretend to be a close friend who is concerned about her and offer to remove her from the situation. Your assertiveness in this kind of situation can potentially save another woman from a life-threatening event.

The eighth tip is to request Uber drivers to wait until you have safely found your house keys and opened your door before they can leave. Predators are trained to take advantage of every second that they have to attack their victim, thus, a few seconds spent trying to find your keys can be enough time for the predator to approach. It is always advised to have a pair of eyes watching over you while you maneuver in public spaces. The ninth tip is to follow a man to the bar when they offer to buy you a drink. Free drinks offered in social settings can be used to drug or take advantage of women. If you decide to accept a free drink, insist on watching it prepared by the bartender. In this way, you will know who made it and what went into the drink when it was being prepared.

The tenth tip is to turn off the music from your headphones when you are walking alone. Part of feeling safe is to be aware of your surroundings and notice any sudden changes or unfamiliar occurrences. Music can become a distraction, preventing you from assessing signals of danger. Remaining vigilant in social settings is a superpower because it makes you less vulnerable to sudden attacks. I find it also beneficial to record how I feel when visiting certain places, and noting places that made me feel uncomfortable or threatened in some way. I will usually avoid travelling to those places, even when others choose to go. My intuition is my best friend in guiding me toward social settings that are empowering and offer me an enriching experience, while avoiding those social settings that make me feel powerless or afraid.

Part of unsubscribing to the narratives of fear which are perpetuated in our society, is to go out of our way to feel safe in our bodies and environments. Feeling safe in who we are and where we find ourselves in our lives will give us the confidence to seize opportunities, travel outside of our comfort zones, take calculated risks, and finally live. Furthermore, the extent to which we display assertiveness in our personal and professional lives will depend on how safe we feel in our own homes or work environments. It is challenging to convince a fearful woman of her own power when the systems in her life reflect her powerlessness. Therefore, removing yourself from threatening environments, people, and places should be your first mission before you can practice displaying confidence and assertiveness. Living under a threatening environment will make a mockery of your positive progress, as it continues to reinforce your perceived weakness.

Conclusion

Many women believe that confidence is a learned skill that only a few courageous enough to learn it can have. The truth however is that confidence is a natural human quality that we are born with, which has led to the survival of the human race. If confidence was optional, survival would be optional too. What is less obvious for many afflicted women to see, is that their ability to endure through suffering or injustice requires a certain level of confidence—otherwise, women would have perished under the systematic oppression that has prevailed throughout centuries of history. This perspective on confidence is different from the widely recognized depiction of confidence being a display of audaciousness or passion.

I accept both ideas, however, I am encouraged to argue that true confidence is the kind found in women that have experienced rock bottom and through confident assertions, have found ways of overcoming their pain and misfortune. It is the kind of confidence you would find in a woman whose job was to make tea for her male colleagues before meetings and in a matter of years, was able to sit at the head of the boardroom table, commanding the meeting. This kind of confidence is underrated because it requires a deep acceptance of who you are, as well as accepting your starting point in life. Those women who display true confidence are not ashamed of where their journey began, because they realize that it will not end in the same position.

This book has highlighted the importance of confidence and assertiveness on a woman's road to success at home and in the office. With so many hurdles and opposition that women have to face, success is not as straightforward as it is for men. Before we can aim for success, we need to first understand the many ways which we have been physically, psychologically, and systematically excluded from participating in our society. Gender inequality and discrimination continues to create barriers inhibiting the access to certain positions of power for women. There are still many hoops that we need to jump through before we can receive the same acknowledgement and rewards as men in the workplace. The evidence of gender inequality and sexist practices and policies has created a confidence gap, which makes us doubt or undermine our own performance at work (even when we are high performers).

The confidence gap further perpetuates gender inequality because the negative perceptions of performance at work make women reluctant to ask for promotions or salary increases. In other words, women in the workplace face external environmental barriers, as well as internal psychological barriers. Becoming confident is therefore a necessary quality to relearn because it resolves how a woman sees herself, which empowers her to see opportunities for growth in her environment. Without confidence and assertiveness, women will find it difficult to engage in effective communication with their peers—communication which can build relationships and unlock opportunities.

The fear of speaking up against injustices at work or unfair practices that affect work performance is unhealthy. It is only through healthy and assertive communication that women can begin educating men on their experience of work and how male privilege perpetuates discrimination against women at work. Passive or aggressive communication fails in how it delivers a message; the message either comes across as unclear or dominating. Both messages will not assist women in reclaiming their power in the workplace and convincing men to listen. Instead, assertive communication which seeks to create a win-win outcome for both parties will influence positive transformation at work.

You Were Born to Lead

Leadership does not need to be profiled as a man's role. Effective leadership at home, work, or within your community requires two things—confidence and assertiveness. Contrary to popular belief, you do not need to be aggressive in order to be respected as a good leader. Rather, your team members or family are looking for someone who has a vision and can positively share it with them. Your great visions on how to raise your children, invest money, make the workflow in your organization run more smoothly, or make your community safer to live in will go unnoticed if you cannot share them. Leadership therefore boils down to your courage and commitment to share who you are with others confidently and assertively.

You won't find anything worth sharing if you are filled with self-doubt or negative self-talk. Your mind will either be your friend or foe in helping you outgrow negative thought patterns, habits, and stepping into the fullness of your power as a woman. You can regulate your mind through adopting positive thinking, however, the best cure for a rebellious mind is to shift the narrative that you have created about your own life. Instead of believing in your inadequacies, choose to believe in your limitless potential. This means that you don't need evidence of greatness in your life before you believe that you deserve it and can therefore achieve it. You are full of pure potential that is found within you; all of the goals that you will ever achieve lie dormant in your mind every day.

It is time to wake up to your potential and seize every trace of goodness in your environment. Choose to be a phenomenal mother, phenomenal employee, and a phenomenal friend. It is never too late to rewrite the narrative that you have for your life in order for it to reflect your hopes instead of your fears. Your new narrative does not need to emphasize your shortcomings or the many failures that you have experienced in your life. Rather, it should emphasize your value, built through countless moments of courageous effort. You are strong because you have survived what was manufactured to break you down. This strength therefore makes you more valuable than gold. There are many ways of using this inherent strength to create a positive momentum of progress in your life, powering a virtuous cycle of goodness.

I hope that this book has inspired you to stand up against gender inequality in your own life and refuse to live as a second class citizen. I am certain that your commitment to following some of the guidelines and practices highlighted in this book will provide you with the necessary conviction to transform every relationship in your life. I am also certain that at this point, you are aware of what you deserve and the kind of life that will bring you much needed happiness. With your new found confidence and assertiveness, begin to shape your reality according to this new blueprint that you have envisioned. I know you have the power to do it, because many women before you have done it and have lived to tell the testimonies of their emancipation. The only favor that I ask of you, is to take the knowledge and wisdom that you have learned from this book, and empower another woman about their inner confidence and assertiveness.

References

Achor, S. (2019, September 23). *The 'Virtuous Cycle': How to Create Compounding Successes.* SUCCESS. https://www.success.com/virtuous-cycle/

Are there any differences in the development of boys' and girls' brains? (2019). ZERO TO THREE. https://www.zerotothree.org/resources/1380-are-there-any-differences-in-the-development-of-boys-and-girls-brains

Assertiveness Quotes (94 quotes). (n.d.). Goodreads https://www.goodreads.com/quotes/tag/assertiveness

Ballantyne, C. (2018, June 11). *The Virtuous Cycle of Success.* Early To Rise. https://www.earlytorise.com/the-virtuous-cycle-of-success/

Belephant, T. (2017). *Communication Styles: Increasing Awareness Between Genders in the Workforce.* https://opus.govst.edu/cgi/viewcontent.cgi?article=1336&context=capstones

Bouley, J. (2017, June 1). *How to be confident and assertive during job interviews.* Hospitalrecruiting.com. https://www.hospitalrecruiting.com/blog/3901/how-to-be-confident-and-assertive-during-job-interviews/

Browning, F. (2015, April 29). *Survival Secrets: What Is It About Women That Makes Them More Resilient Than Men?* Cal Alumni Association. https://alumni.berkeley.edu/california-magazine/just-in/2015-04-30/survival-secrets-what-it-about-women-makes-them-more

Center for Clinical Interventions. (2005). *Improving Self-Esteem Module 5: Negative Self-Evaluations*. Centre for Clinical Interventions. https://www.cci.health.wa.gov.au/-/media/CCI/Consumer-Modules/Improving-Self-Esteem/Improving-Self-Esteem---05---Negative-Self-Evaluations.pdf

Cherry, K. (2007, April 22). *Self Efficacy: Why Believing in Yourself Matters*. Verywell Mind; Verywellmind. https://www.verywellmind.com/what-is-self-efficacy-2795954

Christian, L. (2019, August 22). *Understanding the 4 Communication Styles: What's Yours?* SoulSalt. https://soulsalt.com/communication-style/

Citroner, G. (2020, March 10). *You Probably Touch Your Face 16 Times an Hour: Here's How to Stop*. Healthline; Healthline Media. https://www.healthline.com/health-news/how-to-not-touch-your-face

Clarke, L. (2019, June 5). *Do Women Hold Themselves Back in the Workplace?* Lawyer Monthly | Legal News Magazine. https://www.lawyer-monthly.com/2019/06/do-women-hold-themselves-back-in-the-workplace/

Clear, J. (2013, April 11). *The Science of Developing Mental Toughness in Health, Work, and Life*. James Clear. https://jamesclear.com/mental-toughness

Compoint, T. (2019, March 5). *10 key barriers for gender balance*. Déclic International. https://declicinternational.com/key-barriers-gender-balance-2/

Daniels, E. (2018, May 1). *50 Empowering Quotes for Women | ProFlowers*. ProFlowers Blog. https://www.proflowers.com/blog/empowering-quotes

Daniels, L.-A. (2017, August 17). *#WomensMonth: 8 things women just do better than men*. Iol https://www.iol.co.za/news/opinion/womensmonth-8-things-women-just-do-better-than-men-10800914

Deodhar, N. (2017, October 23). *As #MeToo gains momentum, let's look at how people view feminism and male privilege in urban India - India News , Firstpost.* Firstpost. https://www.firstpost.com/india/as-metoo-gains-momentum-many-unhappy-about-few-privileged-feminists-starting-gender-war-4166371.html

Dienstman, A. M. (2018, August 9). *How Taking Risks Can Lead You to a Better Life - Goodnet.* Goodnet. https://www.goodnet.org/articles/how-taking-risks-lead-you-to-better-life

Eating Disorders Victoria. (2018). *Home | Eating Disorders Victoria.* Eatingdisorders.Org.Au. https://www.eatingdisorders.org.au/

Empowering women | STOP HUNGER. (n.d.). Stop Hunger. http://www.stop-hunger.org/home/priorite-femmes/lautonomisation-des-femmes.html

Experteer Magazine. (2018, November 28). *Being assertive in the workplace - Experteer Magazine.* Experteer Magazine. https://us.experteer.com/magazine/being-assertive-in-the-workplace/

Faith. (2016, January 14). *The need for assertiveness in the workplace.* Skills Portal. https://www.skillsportal.co.za/content/need-assertiveness-workplace

Garner, E. (2012). *Assertiveness: Re-claim Your Assertive Birthright.* Ventus Publishing ApS. http://www.gesp.ipg.pt/files/assertiveness.pdf

Gender and the environment: What are the barriers to gender equality in sustainable ecosystem management? (2020, January 23). IUCN. https://www.iucn.org/news/gender/202001/gender-and-environment-what-are-barriers-gender-equality-sustainable-ecosystem-management

Gopalakrishnan, M. (2018, November 5). *Dear Men, #MeToo Is Not A War Against You.* Feminism In India. https://feminisminindia.com/2018/11/06/me-too-war-men/

Gqola, P. D. (2019, September 19). *The patriarchy expects you to follow these scripts.* New Frame. https://www.newframe.com/the-patriarchy-expects-you-to-follow-these-scripts/

Hama, T. (2017, June 6). *Do you suffer from "Pull Her Down" (Phd) Syndrome? | All4Women.* All 4 Women. https://www.all4women.co.za/1111821/leisure/inspiring/suffer-pull-phd-syndrome

Harry. (n.d.). *Being "Assertive" in Job Interviews.* The Wise Job Search. http://www.thewisejobsearch.com/2010/10/being-assertive-in-job-interviews.html

Jensen, L. (2015, July 29). *17 Ways That Science Proves Women Are Superior To Men.* Thought Catalog; Thought Catalog. https://thoughtcatalog.com/lorenzo-jensen-iii/2015/07/17-ways-that-science-proves-women-are-superior-to-men/

John, A. (2018, November 24). *What are the benefits and advantages of Positive thinking?* Medium. https://medium.com/@likhithak.dmp/what-are-the-benefits-and-advantages-of-positive-thinking-cd46ba3154c4

Jones, A. (2019, November 25). *Bridging the confidence gap at work means forming new habits.* Www.Ft.Com. https://www.ft.com/content/8ea25414-07be-11ea-a958-5e9b7282cbd1

Kay, K., & Shipman, C. (2014). *The Confidence Gap The Confidence Gap.* https://theavarnagroup.com/wp-content/uploads/2015/11/The-Confidence-Gap-The-Atlantic.pdf

Lauren Alexis Fisher. (2017, March 8). *35 Empowering Feminist Quotes from Inspiring Women.* Harper's BAZAAR; Harper's BAZAAR.

https://www.harpersbazaar.com/culture/features/a4056/empowering-female-quotes/

Le, E. (2018, June 22). *Why Women's Stronger Emotional Intelligence Is a Big Leadership Advantage.* EVE. https://www.eveprogramme.com/36302/emotional-intelligence-monica-thakrar/

Lucas, J. (n.d.). *Assertiveness for women.* Www.Psychotherapist-Cambridge.Com. Retrieved August 7, 2020, from https://www.psychotherapist-cambridge.com/articlefive.php

Marinos, S. (2016, June 17). *6 steps to better body image.* Bodyandsoul; bodyandsoul.com.au. https://www.bodyandsoul.com.au/diet/body-confidence/6-steps-to-better-body-image/news-story/59c6fe2456a1a3e2c933d8ea0e2fd668

McCrimmon, M. (n.d.). *self-esteem-stories | Self Esteem.* Leadersdirect.Com. http://www.leadersdirect.com/self-esteem-stories

Mind Tools Content Team. (2009). *Body Language Picking Up and Understanding Nonverbal Signals.* Mindtools.Com. https://www.mindtools.com/pages/article/Body_Language.htm

Mindell, M. (2018, September 14). *11 Ways Women Can More Assertive in the Workplace.* Www.Oswaldcompanies.Com. https://www.oswaldcompanies.com/media-center/11-ways-to-be-more-assertive-in-the-workplace-womens-leadership-forum-2018/

9 Advantages of Assertiveness. (2017, June 8). The Three Insights to Your Purposeful Life. https://threeinsights.net/book/9-advantages-of-assertiveness/

Nugumanov, M. (2019, November 8). *A Study Shows That Women Have a Better Memory Than Men, Which Explains Why They Always Know*

Where Your Shirt Is. BrightSide — Inspiration. Creativity. Wonder. https://brightside.me/wonder-curiosities/a-study-shows-women-have-a-better-memory-than-men-which-explains-why-she-always-knows-where-your-shirt-is-794702/

Overcoming Negative Body Image. (n.d.). Www.Insearchofmecafe.Com. http://www.insearchofmecafe.com/bodyImage/bodyImage_neglmage.aspx

Pawlowska, E. (2015). *5 Visualization Techniques To Help With Goals, Confidence, And Health | Mercury.* Ilanelanzen.Com. http://www.ilanelanzen.com/mind/5-visualization-techniques-to-help-with-goals-confidence-and-health/

Phillips, N. (2019, March 24). *The things I do as a woman to feel "safe."* Medium. https://medium.com/worthy-perspective/the-things-i-do-as-a-woman-to-feel-safe-41ccae64255c

Quy, L. (n.d.). *Mental Toughness Center.* LaRae Quy. https://laraequy.com/

Rampton, J. (2016, April 8). *How to Know When to Be Assertive With Your Team.* Entrepreneur. https://www.entrepreneur.com/article/273725

Rodger. (n.d.-b). *Acting As If – Life coaching technique to increase confidence.* Www.Lifecoachinghq.Com. http://www.lifecoachinghq.com/posts/acting-as-if-how-to-change-the-way-you-feel.html

The Role Play Interview: Example Exercises With Tips. (2020, June 3). Wikijob.Co.Uk. https://www.wikijob.co.uk/content/interview-advice/interview-types/role-play

Shepard, A. (2019, January 18). *Clearing Mind Chatter With EFT Tapping.* Unconnecting. http://unconnecting.com/all/mbs/clearing-mind-chatter-with-eft-tapping/

6 Reasons Why Women Are Neurologically Wired To Be Leaders. (2018, March 26). The Health Loft. https://www.thehealthloft.ca/6-reasons-why-women-are-neurologically-wired-to-be-leaders/#:~:text=A%20Women

Solomon, M. S. (2016, June 10). *10 Tips for Conveying Confidence - Fake It Till You Make It.* HuffPost. https://www.huffpost.com/entry/10-tips-for-conveying-con_b_10362606

Starak, Z. (2010, August 4). *How to Communicate Assertively in Your Relationship.* AIPC Article Library. https://www.aipc.net.au/articles/how-to-communicate-assertively-in-your-relationship/

State of Victoria. (2012). *Self esteem.* Vic.Gov.Au. https://www.betterhealth.vic.gov.au/health/healthyliving/self-esteem

Strube, E. (2016, August 14). *Want To Be More Assertive? Use A LADDER!* Www.Linkedin.Com. https://www.linkedin.com/pulse/want-more-assertive-use-ladder-erin-strube#:~:text=The%20LADDER%20Model

Swart, T. (2018, March 27). *The 4 Underlying Principles Of Changing Your Brain.* Forbes. https://www.forbes.com/sites/taraswart/2018/03/27/the-4-underlying-principles-to-changing-your-brain/#236e8da15a71

Tagg, T. (2015, December 26). 4 Mind Shifts That Turn Adversity Into Advantage. *HuffPost.* https://www.huffpost.com/entry/4-mind-shifts-that-turn-adversity-into-advantage_b_8795674?guccounter=1&guce_referrer=aHR0cHM6Ly93d3cuZ29vZ2xlLmNvbS8&guce_referrer_sig=AQAAAJOiTP0d-0qq4tXWYBRXrm_0r7jKgsrso854H8IBHQEkTg4iHl-Hw38Xf-qoK1lc7Rp2vH17LswooxeVWHChqZS7kQWB8ASS8G6psY

w43tleotjDa2e74hCf18dG7Z08mtYS-
y5D7gKjwBP4uX20msmBI4JPhrfa6u35hXIinAs-

Taylor, S. (2012, August 30). *Why Men Oppress Women*. Psychology Today. https://www.psychologytoday.com/us/blog/out-the-darkness/201208/why-men-oppress-women

Vivyan, C. (2009). *Assertiveness*. Get Self Help. https://www.getselfhelp.co.uk/docs/Assertiveness.pdf

What Is EFT Tapping? 5-Step Technique for Anxiety Relief. (2017, December 1). Healthline. https://www.healthline.com/health/eft-tapping#technique

Wise, A. (2019, January 16). *Things Women Do Better Than Men*. Make Your Relationship Work. https://www.beliefnet.com/columnists/makeyourrelationshipwork/2019/01/things-women-better-men.html